Life: Styled by Willie

Life: Styled by Willie

Willorene Morrow

WRITER'S PROOF

Athens, Georgia

Published by Writer's Proof,
an imprint of Miglior Press

Athens, Georgia

www.migliorpress.com

A portion of the profits from this book will be donated
to the Muscular Dystrophy Association's ALS Division.
To make an additional donation, please go to
www.mdanightofhope.org

ISBN 978-0-9822726-2-6

Printed in the United States of America

I dedicate this book to the love of my life, my husband,
Jerry Morrow—my hero.

Also, every mama should be as fortunate as I to have a son
as gifted and special as Duane Morrow—the joy of my life.

A special thanks to Cynthia Wesson for her help
in compiling this book.

And the entire Writer's Proof staff.

Contents

Eula and Cauley Barrow (Mother and Daddy)

Chapter One

In the Beginning

I was born October 6, 1939 in Butler, Georgia, and I certainly made a dramatic entrance. The umbilical cord was wrapped around my neck, and the resulting lack of oxygen turned my tiny body black and blue. The delivery doctor spanked me, but I didn't cry. He popped me a second time and still got no response. He was about to lay my fragile little body on the table, believing I was lost, when he swatted me a third time and I rallied and hollered. And did I holler! I suppose I wanted the world to know I had arrived and was planning to stay.

I heard that story of my refusal to give up all through my childhood and beyond. I've always felt that what happened at my birth is somehow linked to my becoming such an independent person. People have called me tough and told me how amazed they are by my strength and perseverance. Just as I was determined to live right at the beginning of life, so I've been determined throughout this life to make the best of things and to create my own style in life. Another important factor is that I come from an agricultural family, and we made our own way. I was not used to seeing paychecks come into the house. I have followed that way of life. I never have had a paycheck from someone. I've always worked for myself.

I never knew either of my grandfathers. Granddaddy Barrow, my daddy's father, passed away before I was born. He was a farmer. I really don't know much about him. I did know my daddy's mama, Alice Schrimpshire. She was a real sweet lady. I'm convinced the definition of grandmother was based on her. She was a true grandmother. She had the most beautiful short, silver hair and would sit in her rocker crocheting the hours away. She ate Tums all the time and, thinking it was candy, I would stand patiently beside her chair until she gave me a few.

My maternal grandmother and her tenth child passed away during the birth, leaving her husband, Howard Underwood, to raise their surviving nine young daughters. A few years later, he married Maggie Mae and together they had two sons and a daughter. Their two young sons were four and two when Howard was killed. He met a sad end. My mother was just eighteen. Grandfather Underwood was a McNess door-to-door salesman, marketing cleaning products and extracts and flavorings, among other household items. One night, in the driving rain, he spotted two young men well known to him walking down the muddy road. Being the good-natured soul that he was, he stopped and offered them a ride. They rewarded his gesture of kindness by robbing and murdering him. The book *Murder at the County Line* by Avoline Bloodworth recounts this life-altering tragedy in detail. The men who murdered him were the last two men to be hung by the state of Georgia.

I was born into the agricultural family of Robert Cauley Barrow and Eula J. Underwood. They lived in Potterville,

Georgia, a small community about four miles outside of Reynolds. They had two boys, Kenneth, fourteen years old when I was born, and Robert, two years younger, and two daughters, Jeannette, ten years old when I was born and Betty Wray, five years younger than Jeannette. As a child, when I was not being carried on Jeannette's hip as her make-believe baby doll, I would follow her everywhere. I referred to Jeannette as "Mama," and called my mother "Mother." Even as a very young child, I was keenly aware that Betty Wray was mother's pet.

Work was a family affair. When Daddy was farming with the mules, my brothers always farmed with him. That was the way it was. We all helped wherever we could to make our life successful and productive. When Daddy plowed close to the house on hot summer days and he came close to the end of a row, I'd carry ice water out for him and the men to drink. By the time I was in high school, Daddy was farming with tractors.

&a.

My mother was a very strict disciplinarian. She had definite rules for her children, especially her girls. To begin with, we were never allowed to wear shorts or pants. (When I was in high school, though, for some unknown reason, she suddenly allowed me to begin wearing pants.) Dancing was never allowed, nor could "her girls" wear makeup. She taught us how to work, and she worked us hard. Obedience was the name of the game and absolutely mandatory in our house. Her mandates were met without a moment of resistance, hesitation, or even question.

When any one of us was daringly disobedient, we experienced the "wrath of Eula," and not a single one of us wanted that experience! She would make us go and pick our own switch for a whipping; it had better be a "long, keen one" or you received a double dose of her wrath. My sisters and I were not allowed to swim, but my brothers were. She would take us down to the pond that bordered our property and allow us to wade in the water in the heat of the summertime. I tease everybody now, telling them mother told us we had to learn how to swim before we could swim. Of course, my grandchildren think that is funny. They can't quite grasp the notion that I don't swim, even today.

We lived on a farm about a mile from an area referred to as "The Village." Bibb Manufacturing Company, a local cotton mill, had built homes for their employees to rent and, thus, developed this small community. All the children in the area attended grammar school in Potterville. Schools during that time were divided into two grade classifications. Grammar school was first through seventh grade. High school was eighth through twelfth. My first year of school, we had to walk the one mile to school. Of course, my brothers and sisters had been walking that mile all those years before I came along and started school, but after my first year, we all had a brand new school bus. Things were beginning to improve in my life. As I remember, by the time I graduated from the seventh grade, I was the valedictorian. The competition was stiff. There were five classmates that year vying for the honor.

Daddy bought our first refrigerator when I was in high school. Prior to that, we used an icebox to preserve foods. The ice man would come to the house once a week or so, delivering large blocks of ice to be placed in the icebox to keep foods from spoiling. Before the icebox, we used tin wash tubs and wrapped the ice blocks in croker sacks, burlap bags used to store feed for the farm animals. The sacks slowed the melting process, but not by much.

Another difference between my early life and life today is that back then, we had to churn cream to make our butter. After my sisters left home, I became the resident churner and churned the cream on a daily basis. I hated to churn! I tried my best to knock the bottom out of that churn by banging the churning stick down hard, but I never succeeded.

I knew just how long it took for that cream to turn to butter: exactly twenty minutes. It seemed like an eternity. Mother would pour the milk into a pan and then put it in the ice box to wait for the cream to rise to the top. Afterward, she would scrape the cream off the top of the milk and put it in the churn, waiting for it to "clabber." The leftover milk was our sweet milk to drink, same thing as the milk we drink today, only now it is pasteurized. Our buttermilk came from allowing the milk to barely sour and thicken to create the small curds. When my good friend Camille, who lived in town, would come out to visit, she loved to churn, so I would let her have at it. As she was churning she would say over and over, "I love to churn. I just love to churn." Being the so-called smarter one, I just loved letting her enjoy her churning. I would laughingly tease her as I reminded her that if she had to do it every day, she wouldn't love it so much. She never minded. Mother would work the water out of that butter and then mold it. She sold milk and butter to several families in town to help with the family expenses.

On Saturday mornings, we were expected to rise early, just like we did when we were going to school. We were not allowed to sleep late. We each had our chores to do, lots of them. I'm not sure what time we got up, but I know it was early. It was still dark. On school days, we must have boarded the school bus around seven thirty, so I'm sure we were up no later than six in the morning. Mother always cooked a big breakfast, making scratch biscuits every morning. Daddy and my brothers needed a hardy breakfast before they went out in the field for the day. We had syrup, biscuits, and plenty of butter. We always sat together as a family at each mealtime, without exception.

We went to the First Baptist Church down at the village. That was our church. There were several other churches in the community, and if any of them were having revivals, we were always there, too. Mother's rule. We had to be there. The doors were open, and we had to be there. We had Thursday-night prayer meetings and then Sunday school and church. Then we had church again Sunday night. The church is still there, though it's changed somewhat. Before Mama and Daddy died, they ended up going to another church, the Mount Olive Freewill Baptist Church. I don't know why they changed to that church later in life, but they did.

Our only method of heat in the house was from the centrally located fireplace. On an unusually bitterly cold day when I was four years old, the fireplace was alive with mesmerizing flames dancing about and sparks flying. Suddenly and without warning, the house was in flames, and we were all running for safety. I remember it vividly. There was panic, screams of terror, and hysteria. To get out of everyone's way, I stood frozen between the two large oak trees in the front yard, holding my baby doll as I watched our house and everything I had known in life burn to the ground.

Uncle Sikes, Mother's paternal uncle, generously insisted that we live in the tenant house on their property until Daddy was able to build our new house. Uncle Sikes and Aunt Mattie had eleven children. Most had grown up and moved from home at that time, although a few of them were still living at home. It was fun having new playmates. Between working the farm and building our new house with Robert and Kenneth's help, there was a great deal of activity. The new house was smaller, and we all adjusted. The front of the house had no steps leading to the door. I remember we laid down an old railroad crosstie outside the door to use as a doorstep.

In the pasture of the old house, Daddy had a sugarcane mill where he ground the cane. Then he cooked it in a vaporizer and made sugarcane syrup. Boy, was it good on good old homemade biscuits. There was nothing better than coming in hungry from school and finding a cold, leftover biscuit, boring a hole in the middle of the biscuit with your finger and pouring some of that good sweet syrup in the hole. Now, that was a good after school snack, almost as good as a cold baked sweet potato.

Daddy—my hero (Cauley Barrow)

Jeanette, me, and Belinda

The Barrow family: (seated) Daddy and Mama; (middle row) me, Jeanette, and Betty Wray; (back row) Kenneth and Robert

Life-long best friends: Camille, me, and Betty

My 70th birthday: me, Kenneth, and Betty Wray

Also in this pasture were lots of grapevines that produced lots of good fruit. It was good to eat the grapes right off the vines or to use them in pies or jellies or preserves. Mother made delicious pies each season, and her scuppernong cobbler was known throughout the community.

I certainly don't want to forget to mention the good plum trees that grew along the banks of the road leading up to our house. I love good green plums with salt. I was always told those good green plums would give me a stomach ache, but to this day I still eat them and I've never once had a stomach ache.

There were hickory nut and black walnut trees on the farm as well. No taste in the world can compare to fresh walnuts, but they are hard to crack, and it takes lots of work. In the summertime, mother always canned our vegetables, enough to last the family through a cold winter season and into the next spring. The concept of frozen foods simply did not exist at that time. There were huge washtubs of butterbeans, peas, snap beans, and corn for us to shell and shuck as we sat under the mulberry trees preparing the vegetables for her to can. I shelled so many butterbeans and peas I thought my fingers would fall off; they were so sore each season.

Some of our other chores included the weekly ironing for the entire family, along with mopping and waxing the linoleum floors. We had to hoe the grass in the yard at the front and back doors and then sweep that area with dog fennel and reed cane. Mother would tie some of the dog fennel together for us to sweep the yard. To make the straw brooms that she used to sweep inside the house, we would go across the road and cut some of that straw. You see it today on the side of the roads out in the country. For a long time, we didn't have a lawn mower, and each of the girls took turns cutting the grass with a sling blade. Daddy finally bought a lawn mower, but it didn't have a motor. We had to walk behind it and push it to make the blades rotate. My brothers worked in the field with Daddy, but he would not allow the girls to work in the fields. It was considered men's work, and the "sisters" stayed home to do the "women's work" with Mother.

Daddy raised hogs and cows. He would slaughter some of them, and that gave us plenty of meat. My daddy was a neat guy. All he had to do was point his finger at us, and we knew we'd better straighten up pronto. He let Mother do the spankings. He would always tell us that work never killed anyone. We definitely got our work ethic from him. He and my brothers, Kenneth and Robert, farmed together. They always planted cotton, and when cotton-picking time came, I would beg to go to the field and pick cotton. Daddy didn't usually let the girls in the field, but he would let me pick for awhile. I always wanted to pick a hundred pounds in a day, but I never seemed to get over sixty pounds.

My daddy was one of those laid-back, easygoing, good people, like my second husband, Jerry. Jerry was just so laid-back and good, just a good, good person. I always said I wanted to be like my daddy. Mother was much more high-strung than Daddy. As I've said, she was a very strict disciplinarian.

I used to run and get in his lap to get away from her. I'd run, jump in his lap, and say, "Daddy, save me, save me."

He would hold me high in the air and say, laughing, "Get away, Eula, get away." He loved to tease and hassle my mother, and it would tickle him to no end to see how frustrated she would become. As I've said, the house had no internal heating system like houses today, just the fireplace. It wasn't until I was in high school that we had gas space heaters. Daddy would sit by the fire just long enough to warm himself, and then to aggravate mother, he would say to her, "I'm hot, Eula. Tell me to move, tell me to move."

She would snap back, "I'm not going to tell you to move. If you don't know any better than to move when you get hot, then just sit there and burn up." He would laugh and laugh.

❧

The luxury of today's modern plumbing was also nonexistent in our house. There was no running water in the entire house. For the most part, we entered and exited from the back door, next to which was a washstand with a bowl of water for us to use to wash our hands as we came in the house. We did not use paper towels. We used the empty flour sacks as dish cloths, and they were good ones, too. At dishwashing time, after boiling the water to wash the dishes (and drinking glasses, utensils, and cooking pots), we'd have one pan for washing and one pan for rinsing. We used additional flour sacks for drying.

Drawing our water was a three-stage process. Our well

was about fifty feet from the back door. First, we lowered the bucket with a heavy rope into the depths of the well to fill it with water. That was the easiest stage. Next, someone lifted the full bucket to the top either by hand or a crank: hard work resulting in strong muscles. The weight of a full bucket of water being carried into the house made the fifty or so feet seem far more treacherous than it was in reality. Years later, this well went dry and Daddy had to dig a new well. He installed a cast-iron hand pump that drew the water from the bottom of the well and poured it directly into a bucket placed under the spout of the hand pump.

By today's standards, bathing at our farm was a unique experience. Our bathtubs were actually large aluminum wash tubs, the ones we used when washing clothes by hand. In the summertime, we would put those wash tubs in the sunshine in the back yard before filling them with the cold water from the well. That way the sunshine could warm it a little before we slipped into the tub. Can you just imagine sitting outside in the fresh air in a tub of fresh well water, feeling the summer breeze blowing? That was one of the many joys of country living. During the winter months, we would heat the water on the stove, pouring it into the tubs that had been brought inside.

There was no bathroom in our house, a lack that required my family, like so many others in the country, to use an outhouse behind the house. We used pages from old catalogs or magazines as toilet paper. Only people with money and indoor plumbing had regular toilet paper. This was always embarrassing to me, especially when I would invite my girlfriends to spend the night, but it never bothered them. They thought it was a novelty. I was embarrassed to death. We had no air conditioning, either, and the house had a tin roof, so it became extremely hot in the summertime. We slept with all of the windows and doors open. Try doing that today!

When I would have spend-the-night parties with my girlfriends from town, Mother would always come into our party to read from the scriptures and pray with us. Some of the girls just loved asking her questions about the Bible. Of course, as she would be reading to us, I would be thinking, "Y'all don't need to be doing this. We need to be playing." There was Camille, Betty, and me: we were the closest of friends. Camille lived in Reynolds, and I always called her the "City Girl." Betty lived out on the other side of town on a farm and had a bathroom in her house. A cousin of mine, Jane, lived close to the village about a mile from my house. At one time, her daddy ran the office for the cotton mill, but when he bought the five-and-dime store in town, they moved to town. I loved going to visit Jane once they moved because we could ride our bicycles on concrete, which was "big time" back then. Where I lived, there were only dirt roads to ride on.

❧

As I grew older, I remember there being a theater in Reynolds. There's not one there today. I remember going to the movies on occasion, but I don't remember any particular movie. With no television, we listened to the radio a lot. As a family, we would sit around the radio on Saturday nights, listening to music. I don't remember when Mother and Daddy bought a television, but I'm sure we had a black and white one when I graduated from school.

Once chores were finished, playtime was always enjoyable. I loved to play with my playhouse and dolls. When Betty Wray was still home, she and I would play jump board, seesaw, hopscotch, and make walkie-talkies out of cans and strings. To play jump board, you needed a cinder block and a long board; a person would stand on one end of the board while the other person would jump on the opposite end, causing the person standing on the original end to fly into the air. When that person comes down and lands on the board, the first jumper flies laughing into the air. Today's children know nothing about those kinds of games and toys. We had to make our own toys then, or they were handed down, like the bicycle I received from my sister Betty Wray when she no longer would ride. There were no Toys-R-Us stores. The rare toys which were bought from stores were usually ordered through the Sears and Roebuck catalog and then picked up at a local Sears.

I remember another old game called "pulling the rosin string." Uncle Johnny Kimble was one of my Grandmother Minnie's brothers and would stay at our house often. He treated us like his own children, loving us and playing jokes on us all the time. It was great sport for him. He would get rosin from a pine tree and then tie a string around a nail, hammering the nail into the weatherboard of the house. He would then pull the rosin on the string. It sounded like the whole side of the house was coming down. He knew it would scare us to death, and he'd just laugh a huge belly laugh. He used to tell me he would give me a nickel if I would be quiet for five minutes. I don't think I ever earned that nickel.

Sometimes it was Mother or some of the older children who would play jokes on me. In the heat of the summer, they would drape sheets over their heads and walk slowly past the wide-open windows, making crazy noises, scaring the be-jeebers out of me. I'd run to the safety of my big sisters or whoever was available. Other times, we would spend hours outside playing hide and seek.

In the summertime, while we were out of school, the girls were responsible for keeping the house and cooking while mother sewed; she made most of our clothes. In those days, nothing—and I mean not a thing—went to waste. The chicken-feed sacks came in pretty prints, so women would use these to sew their children's clothes, especially the girls. The dry-goods store in town carried a line of fabrics which were quite popular, and mother created many a dress using the Dan River fabrics.

From as far back as I can remember, one of my favorite jobs was cooking, and mother taught me a lot about the kitchen. I loved it then and still do; it has always been very therapeutic for me. My oldest sister, Jeannette, loved to cook as well, but Betty Wray wasn't the least bit interested. As a child, when I visited my oldest brother, Kenneth, his wife, Ruth, would always welcome me into her kitchen, allowing me to help her cook. When I was just a young girl, she gave me a very small rolling pin that I still have today.

᪥

Throughout my childhood, as each of my sisters and brothers would have willingly confirmed as fact at any time, I loved teasing and aggravating both Jeannette and Betty Wray. About the time I turned seven or eight, Jeannette, being ten years older, was fully interested in boys. I was jealous of the time and attention the boys took away from me. Her boyfriend at the time, Charles Moore, would walk two-plus miles when he came "callin' and a courtin'" to see her on the weekends. It was unheard of for a teenager to own a car back then, and he would travel by foot from his house, around Potterville Lake and another mile or so to our house. At times, as they would be sitting in the living room visiting, I would slip around the corner and begin singing a little tune I made up: "stay all night, stay a little longer, throw off your coat and throw it in the corner, don't see why you don't stay a little longer." It would infuriate Jeannette, but, of course, I thought it was funny. Other times, I would set the alarm clock for a specific time, placing it just outside the door of the room they occupied and wait. My goal was to cause enough grief that he would go home, and I would have my big sister all to myself again. I did not like sharing her attention. I was always pulling pranks when Charles came around. Eventually, they married and had two beautiful girls, Belinda and Debbie. Jeannette passed away July 23, 2006, from a rare form of leukemia, and I still, to this day, miss her very much.

Betty Wray is the striking redhead of our family. I can remember watching her for what seemed like hours, dressing

and preparing for an event and wondering why she was taking so long when I was ready to go in about fifteen minutes.
I would teasingly call her "the primper," but the results were
worth the wait. She is very attractive. After graduating from
high school, she received a business degree from a business
school in Macon, then returned to school to earn her cosme-
tology license. She eventually opened her own beauty salon
in Warner Robins. She had found her niche.

One thing I remember about my brother Robert is that he
always wore a hat everywhere he went. I would slip up behind
him, grab his hat, and run, with him hot on my heels trying
to retrieve his property. More often than not, he wrestled me
to the ground before I surrendered.

Daddy and Robert would use our horses to plow the
fields. Kenneth, on the other hand, used the mules. He did
not like plowing with the horses. There were four horses total; Peggy's color was red roma and her colt, Fannie Mae, was
a blackish red. Daisy was a polka-dot grey with dark circles
which turned white as she matured. Dan was the sandy-col-
ored stud of the quartet. Both Kenneth and Robert loved to
ride the horses in their spare time and would aggressively
race across the fields as they challenged one another, testing
their abilities to arrive at the house first. I was terrified of
the horses and never ever wanted anything to do with what
I perceived as those gigantic monsters. If I was in the yard
playing and saw them racing towards me, I would take off
running just as fast as my little legs could carry me to get into
the house. On more than one occasion, I remember reach-
ing the back door and being in such a panic that I could not

18

get the door open fast enough. I would freeze with terror as they approached, sitting high on the horses' backs, laughing. I never did learn to ride. Maybe my grandchildren will teach me some day, perhaps a goal for my eightieth birthday. (Not a chance!) Later, as Kenneth began to court Ruth, he would ride Fannie Mae, who was no longer a colt, to Ruth's home to call on her.

Kenneth, my older brother, was and always will be my hero. He would allow me to ride with him in his truck. That was a treat, because he would race down the dirt roads where we lived, at what seemed to me a dangerous pace, with me giggling all the way. I was never frightened because to me, he could handle anything.

My sisters and brothers had all attended high school in Butler, Georgia, about eight miles from home. Uncle Sikes would load several of his own children together with my sisters and brothers onto his boarded flatbed truck each day for school. A boy from another family, Alfred Roberson, would drive the packed truck to school each morning and return everyone at the end of the day.

By the time I entered high school, all of the older children had long since graduated, so there was no transportation to Butler High School available. I still thought I should go to school in Butler; after all, my friends were there. Mother had a different idea, and her idea won. She insisted I ride the school bus to the high school in Reynolds. I didn't want to go and was very upset in the beginning. I knew no one in the new school, and most of the girls didn't want to have anything to do with a farm girl from Potterville. After a few weeks, however, I began to fit right in. Camille Cook, Betty Childre, and I quickly became inseparable. We were the best of friends and have remained so throughout our lives. I liked most of my new teachers, and I think they liked me as well. Mr. Joiner, the principal, was well known for giving few passing grades at the end of the school year. He liked for you to attend summer school to receive your passing score.

&.

After Daddy retired from farming, sometime in the very late '70s, he began having periodic chest pains and difficulty catching his breath. It eventually became severe enough that he was rushed by ambulance to the hospital in Macon more than once. The doctors could not find the cause. The pain continued and increased. A doctor in Thomaston did a series of tests and diagnosed that Daddy had at some time suffered a hernia, probably from the years of pushing, pulling, and lifting on the farm. His intestines had bulged through the hernia and wrapped around his heart, gradually constricting more and more of his airflow and literally suffocating him to death. After several more years of continued suffering, Daddy passed away on August 19, 1983.

Mother continued to live in their home until we moved her to a nursing facility in Butler. Visiting her in the later years of her life was difficult; it was not until we spoke that she could recognize who was by her side, having become blind from glaucoma. At age ninety-four, her mind was sharp as a tack. She could tell us anything we wanted to know and could think to ask her. She was remarkable. The day she passed, all five of her children were gathered around her bed, listening to her as she sang several of her favorite hymns. She never missed a single word or verse. We each knew she was tired and ready to join Daddy, but more importantly, she was waiting to meet her Lord and Savior, Jesus Christ. As her breathing became more labored, she began singing in whispered tones her all-time favorite hymn, "Amazing Grace," and she calmly moved into the presence of our Lord. What a sweet moment and comforting memory this has been throughout the years since her passing on July 3, 2000. Within less than four months, our family was jolted by another shock, the loss of our brother Robert to emphysema on October 24, 2000.

Chapter Two

A New Life

As a senior in high school, I read the book *The Power of Positive Thinking* by Norman Vincent Peale, and that book really made a tremendous impact on my life. It really, really made sense to me. It takes just as much energy to be negative as it does to be positive, so why not choose to be positive? I get up with the attitude that it's going to be a great day. I've also lived by a verse in the Bible, Philippians 4:13: "I can do all things through Christ which strengthens me." I stop and think, "Can I do this? Yes, I can do all things through Christ which strengthens me. Sure, I can do it." If anybody else can do it, I can do it, can't I?

So, this philosophy helped guide me in my choices. When I graduated from high school, I had decided that I wanted to be a hairdresser. I would cut anybody's hair who would let me when I was in school. I did my own hair all the time. When I asked Daddy for permission to go, he asked me if I was going to stay for the duration of the course. Back then, the training took six months. At one point, my sister Betty Wray had gotten Daddy to send some money to a business school in Atlanta for her. She was planning on completing a program there, and then she backed out after a few days, deciding to go to the Business Training Institute in Macon, instead. Daddy lost some of the money, so he asked me if I was going to stay in school, and I said, "Yes, sir. If I go, I'm staying." And so I stayed and was true to my word.

Back then, for that six-month course, it cost about $600, a huge sum of money in those days. After I left school and started working, I started saving money to give Daddy. That Christmas I gave him a shirt, and I pinned six one-hundred-dollar bills on it and thanked him for my course. It meant a lot to me that he had been willing to let me go and paid all of the tuition. He was sure surprised, but at the same time proud of what I had accomplished.

My mother went to a hair dresser in Butler, which was about eight miles from Reynolds. Her name was Bernaline. She was very good at her trade. She had attended beauty school in Atlanta at the Artistic Beauty School. When I got out of high school, she volunteered to carry Mother and me up to Artistic to get me enrolled. I was this little country girl. I'd never been to Atlanta but twice in my life, and that was with Mother on a shopping trip. I don't know how I had the courage to say, "Yeah, I want to go to Atlanta." Actually, I'm surprised I didn't go to Macon to beauty school. Ultimately, Artistic was the right school for me.

While I was in school, I lived in a church-sponsored home for business girls at the corner of Piedmont and 14th Street. It was a sort of dormitory for girls. My roommate happened to be Allethea Smith from Americus, Georgia, who was Rosalyn Carter's sister. Allethea had a car, and, of course, I didn't. So, when she would drive home on the weekends, she would let me ride with her to Butler, and mother would come and pick me up. I rode the trolley down to the beauty school every day. I can remember the first morning, getting that little trolley and being afraid I was going to get on the wrong one. I just made sure I told the trolley driver where I was going and asked him if I was getting on the right one. He was always so sweet to me, making sure I was all right and making sure I knew when to get off. I finally learned my way around, but it was unnerving at first.

While Allethea and I roomed together, there were four or five other girls in adjoining rooms in the same suite. At that time, it was safe to walk the streets of Atlanta at night, and we would often walk down 14th Street and Piedmont Avenue. Once I finished my course of studies in April 1958, I chose to return to Reynolds. My high school sweetheart, Swilling, was waiting for my return, and I wasn't about to disappoint him.

I began my working career at Jeannie's beauty salon. In less than a year, on February 10, 1959, I opened my own beauty shop, the Beauty Nook. It was a very small salon with two hair dryers and two styling/shampoo stations. My niece Merita Carpenter as well as Shelvie Hartley and Ellen Parks worked with me as hair-stylists; they were great. Initially hiring Lynn Underwood as our shampoo girl was a tremendous asset for us, freeing our time to work with more customers. I was taking on a big responsibility at a very young age. I was only twenty.

It was not long before we were outgrowing that little salon. It got to the point on the weekends where women would be standing and waiting for service. Oh, mercy, what a problem to have! So, in 1968, I rented a larger building with ten hair dryers, three shampoo stations, five stylist stations, a kitchenette, and a nice waiting area. Merita and Shelvie were still with me, and Linda Powell and Betty Cox had joined our growing team of stylists. As time passed and business grew, Betty Shiflett, Carlene Albritton, and Amelia Patterson also joined our team.

This was a salon of very pretty girls. One time, a salesman bought a toupee at the beauty supply house in Macon, and they told him he needed to drive to Reynolds, thirty-five miles away, to get it cut and styled. He couldn't believe it and almost decided not to make the drive, but he listened and was cooperative. He told me later when he drove up to that warehouse-looking building that he thought, "What am I doing here?" But when he opened the front door and walked in, he said he thought he'd been ushered into heaven. He said he'd never seen so many pretty girls in one place.

We attracted customers from all around Georgia, including Fort Valley, Perry, Ellaville, Butler, Roberta, Macon, Warner-Robins, Columbus, Oglethorpe, Montezuma, Rupert, Junction City, as well as other neighboring areas. We marketed our services by word of mouth, and we were thriving.

In order to keep up with hair fashion, we made sure to attend a vast assortment of continuing education classes on the weekends. We put a lot of effort into staying up with what was happening in the fashion world, and this was one reason we attracted people from so many different places. Also, I believed in giving service when service was needed. We opened the salon on Saturdays at 4:30 a.m., usually closing around 4:30 p.m. People who worked during the week could get their hair done and then be free the rest of their day off. On weekdays, the doors opened at 7:00 a.m., and we worked until the last person was served, regardless of the time. The customers loved it, and we continued to thrive. We were closed on Sundays and Mondays.

Shelvie made our uniforms, and we were all dressed alike. We even had yellow shoes to match our outfits. I believed in totally looking the part of a stylist and being professional. In other words, when the stylists showed up for work, they'd better make sure they looked the part. They knew my basic rule: Come in with your makeup on and your hair styled. People asked me all the time, "How do you do this at 4:30 a.m.?" And my consistent response was, "Well, we get up at 3:30 a.m."

❦

On Saturday, June 14, 1959, as the hands on the clock struck 3:00 p.m. at the packed Taylor Mill Baptist church in Potterville, Georgia, I became Mrs. Swilling McElmurray. Swilling and I had gone steady throughout high school and were known throughout the community as high school sweethearts. He was the only boy I had ever dated. My sister Betty Wray was my maid of honor, and my bridesmaids were my friends Jeanette, Camille, Betty, and my third cousin, Jane. Their strapless dresses had white lace bodices, pale blue cummerbunds, and full, tea-length chiffon skirts. The cummerbunds paralleled the bright, blue sky of the day. We were honored to have as our pianist Mother's first cousin, "Aunt Winnie" Windham, who was Jane's mother. Aunt Winnie was like a mother to me. My gown was Chantilly lace, long-sleeved and floor length with a train. (It has been packed in storage for decades.)

The day of the wedding, everyone was radiant with smiles as Daddy walked his beaming baby girl down the aisle. Our celebration continued with a reception held in the Community Center building next to the church. The Bakery in Macon delivered our cake early in the day, fortunately! En route to their destination, the original cake broke. Returning to Macon, another cake was quickly prepared, and the trip to deliver the second cake began. This cake broke as well. As frustrated as the bakery delivery drivers were, they again returned to their store for another replacement. The third attempt was the charmer. It arrived well supported and in one piece. It was delicious!

As I hugged and kissed Mother and Daddy goodbye, I vaguely remember "someone" dancing with ecstatic glee, having caught my bouquet as we were leaving to begin our honeymoon in St. Simons Island for a week of newlywed bliss. I couldn't have been happier. I was in love, and life was good!

Swilling and I set up housekeeping, paying $15.00 a month for an apartment at the old homeplace of two spinster sisters, Laurice and Winnie Aultman. Laurice worked at the Citizens State Bank in Reynolds, and I don't remember Winnie working. As husband and wife, we both worked long, hard hours and saved our money. We wanted to improve our lives. We lived there from 1959 until 1962 when we built our own home on Highway 128/Macon Road.

Shelvie, Ann, me. and Merita

Linda Powell, February 1975

Kathy Goddard at work

Me, retro style

Swilling McElmurray, January 1964

As a wedding gift, Swilling's paternal grandmother, Vickie Hartley McElmurray, had given us .83 acres of land to build a house at some point in our future. One Sunday afternoon, I was browsing through the *Macon Telegraph* and found a picture and floor plan of the house I wanted. I loved it and ordered a copy of the prints.

My cousin, Neil Hinton, the son of Mother's sister Velma, was the local contractor in Reynolds at the time, and he built the house. (His brother Coleman's son, Larry, now runs the contracting business.) Needless to say, when we moved from the Aultman Home, we missed Laurice and Winnie for many weeks, as we had enjoyed years of happiness while living there.

Swilling was an only child, born to J. C. and Mattie Emma Mann McElmurray on May 9, 1938. They lived several miles outside of Reynolds. Throughout his school years, he worked with his daddy in the logging business. Once he graduated from high school, he went to work full time with his daddy. Several years after we moved into our own house, he was appointed as the Taylor County Game Warden, and he loved it. He spent most of his time outdoors during the fall and winter months, traveling throughout the county, checking the licenses of local hunters and fishermen. In spring and summer, he patrolled the lakes and rivers, checking for proper safety-jacket use in the boats and verifying that fishermen were abiding by the state limits for numbers of fish caught.

The first five years of our marriage were wonderful; we were young and in love and quickly building a successful life together, but the tide began to turn. He found women, booze, and drugs, partaking of each liberally. I was devastated! I truly loved this man, and I couldn't believe this was happening to our marriage. When I discovered his involvements, I confronted him, and he laughed in my face and admitted it all. We tried many times to work things out, to salvage our marriage. He would claim over and over again he was going to change. He would go to church and ask God to forgive him. Then, after a few weeks he would slip back into the old habits.

My happy married life rapidly disintegrated into a living nightmare, and I was miserable. Also, I had suffered two miscarriages and was heartbroken. Several months after the second miscarriage, I once again discovered, to my delight, that I was pregnant. I quickly learned this was not good news to Swilling, as he became increasingly irrational, mean, and abusive. I was terrified I would not be able to carry this baby to full term. Many a miserable night he would keep me up all night, walking me up and down the hall with his pistol in my back, telling me over and over how he was going to kill me. I was so terrified at times that I wished he would. My misery would have been over, but I had to keep on living for this baby I was carrying.

If I tried to call for help, he would pull the telephone out of the wall. If I tried to get in the car to leave, he'd say, "I'll shoot every tire on the car." Then one Sunday afternoon when I was about eight-months pregnant, we were at his mama and daddy's house; his aunt and uncle were there also. He was very drugged, and they were trying to talk to him. He ran out the front door and shot up in the air twice. His mama thought he'd shot himself. He was always saying he was going to kill himself. But, of course, he just shot up in the air. That's the sort of thing that was going on when I was pregnant, and even after the precious baby came, he still didn't change.

On October 20, 1967, I gave birth to an eight-pound, ten-ounce baby boy. Duane Swilling McElmurray brought a refreshing and cleansing breath together with newfound purpose into my life. He was my miracle, and I knew it! I had now overcome the haunting and seemingly helpless feeling of emptiness, and I wasn't going anywhere.

I had desperately wanted to believe that after Duane was born Swilling would settle down and change, but he didn't. If anything, he slipped further and further into his cruel ways. For the next seven or eight months, I did everything I could think of as I attempted to restore harmony to our marriage and peace to our home. Nothing helped, and I finally came to the realization that it would be up to me to raise this precious child so he could live a happy, safe, and healthy life.

As time went by and Duane got old enough to realize what was going on, he would cry when he saw his daddy mistreat me. That's when I knew I had to get my child out of this environment. I realized that I didn't grow up like this, and I couldn't allow my child to grow up in this kind of environment. I made my decision to file for divorce. My husband's uncle asked the preacher to talk to me and see if he could get me to reconsider. So the preacher called and asked me to come to his office, and I did. (He was new to Reynolds.) When he asked me to have a seat, I said, "Preacher, can I say something first?"

"Sure," he said.

"Since you just moved here," I said, "you don't know me and you don't know my husband, so let me fill you in." Then I told him what the last five or six years had been like.

When I finished, he said, "If anyone ever needed a divorce, it is you.'"

I've always had a strong faith and drew deeply upon this faith as I continued to believe I would get through what I thought to be the toughest experience of my life. The divorce was final on July 6, 1970, bringing a close to the 11 years and 22 days of a tumultuous chapter of my life. Had anyone told me I would have lived under those circumstances for as long as I did, I would have never believed them. Mother and Daddy, being the dedicated Christian people they were, didn't believe in divorce, and I dreaded telling them. I hated for my parents to know things were not going well, and when I finally made the decision to end the marriage, I realized they were keenly aware of far more than I had given them credit for regarding the reality of my marriage. They had been deeply worried about Duane and me, praying for a safe resolution.

The morning of August 2, 2001, I received a call from Duane informing me of a single automobile accident on the back roads of Crawford County that had claimed Swilling's life. He was buried a few days later in the Roberta City Cemetery with Duane in attendance and speaking at the funeral.

Chapter Three

Family Ties

When I served Swilling with the divorce papers, his two uncles threw me a curve ball. Now, Swilling was never where he should be, and so he wasn't there back when we built our house. And when the well digger came to dig the well, half of the pump house ended up on his uncle's land. So, once the divorce papers were served, the uncles put signs all over the pump house that read "Stay Out, Private Property." They told me I had to dig my own well.

Immediately, I called my cousin, Bubba Hinton, who owned a well-digging company in the county. He and Neil Hinton, my house contractor, were brothers. When I asked him how soon he could have me a well dug, he responded by asking me if the next morning would be soon enough. Those were words of hope and exactly what I wanted to hear. The next day I had a well. My initiative and independence shocked Swilling's uncles. Another curve Swilling's family threw me was in reference to the sewage line, which also ran across Uncle Fred's land. He made me change those lines to run down my property line, so they would not infringe on his property.

When the papers were served, Swilling refused to leave that night, so I called his mama and asked her to come spend the night with me. I was not going to stay in the house with him by myself. The next morning, I called my attorney and asked him if I had to stay there and he said no. So I packed a suitcase for myself and one for Duane, and we went and stayed with my cousin Ralph and his wife Irene, who were like brother and sister to me. We stayed with them for three months until the divorce was final. I did not even go back to the house for more clothes during this time.

Mia, Ralph and Irene's daughter, had a great time playing with Duane. Ralph and Irene welcomed us into the love and sanctuary of their home and hearts, never questioning, never judging, and never batting an eye. I felt like we had arrived in heaven. I knew Duane and I were safe at last. Irene and I have always enjoyed each other's company, and Ralph thought no one could cut his hair like me. Their children Kathy and Rudy were also still at home at this time. So, we had quite a full and happy family life going on at the Underwoods.

Having roots in Potterville, where she was born, Irene had grown up in Thomaston where her family moved when she was around age three. Whenever she would return to Potterville to visit relatives, she would go to the "big store" and shop with her aunts. Ralph was about five years her senior and working for his father, who owned the store. This is where they met. After Ralph and Irene were married, they lived in Butler for a while and at one time, they both worked for Uncle Sikes in the grocery store he owned in Potterville. They had three daughters, Lynn, Kathy, Mia, and a son, Rudy. Needless to say, theirs was a very active household. Both Kathy and Lynn worked with me during the summers as shampoo girls at the Beauty Nook. I'm sure, if you ask them, they both

Irene and Ralph Underwood with Mia and Duane

Mia and me, October 2009

would tell you I was very strict, but I taught them to have a good work ethic.

Mia is my godchild; she is two years older than Duane. I've always thought of her as the daughter I never had. She and Duane loved playing together, which helped considerably in softening the blow to our lives, especially for Duane. By the time Duane and I arrived at the Underwood's home, Lynn had already graduated from high school and was working in Washington, D.C.

Eventually, Ralph went to work for an agricultural chemical company as a sales representative. Many a morning as he drove to work, he would stop by the salon, walk in, sit down in a chair next to where I was working, and wait. And wait. And wait. After completing my customer's appointment, I would simply walk over and barely touch his hair while he laughed and laughed. He always said all I had to do was touch—just touch—his hair and it looked better. He told anyone and everyone who would listen that no one could cut his hair like I could. He was such a great guy. Everyone loved him. He passed away far too young at age 49 from a sudden blood clot to his heart. He has been missed by all who knew him. He was like a brother to me.

In reality, Irene and I were cousins by marriage, but we acted more like sisters, thoroughly enjoying our time together. We were always close and trusted each other implicitly. Many years after I stayed with Irene and her family, I called her at the school where she was working and said to her, "Every time you walk by a mirror today, I want you to take a good look at the woman looking back at you. When you get off work, I want you to come to the salon, sit in my chair and read a magazine or the paper without asking me a single question. Complete trust, remember?" She obediently answered, "Yes, ma'am." Later that day, she sat down in my chair with a head of white and gray hair; I turned her away from the mirror and went to work. Hours later, when I turned the chair back to face the mirror, she was a beautiful blonde and loved it! So did her children. Only with Irene could I have been that bold. We had complete faith in each other.

Chapter Four

Surprised

Back in May 1970, My niece, Merita, had been dating my neighbor's son, Wayne Parks. Wayne wanted me to go out with his friend Billy from Warner Robins. When Billy called to ask me for a date on the upcoming Friday night, I gingerly declined, not wanting to offend him. Wayne came into town and stopped by the beauty salon, politely but firmly explaining to me he was not about to accept my answer to his friend. "You are going. Billy can meet us in Macon, and you will ride with me and Merita." What could I say? The arrangements were made.

Later that day, after I put my last customer under the hair dryer, I drove the four miles from the salon to my house to change clothes and get ready for this date. The yard was well lit and the spring sun was still shining when I left, so it never occurred to me to turn on the carport lights when I left. I was about halfway back to the salon when I saw an unfamiliar two-toned green LTD Ford.

Instinctively, I looked in my rear-view mirror, noting the driver had braked but did not stop. I continued on my way, beginning to anticipate the evening. When I arrived, I asked those in the salon if anyone had seen or knew anything about the unfamiliar car, but no one had. I realized much later that the unfamiliar vehicle was the getaway car for burglars who were about to ravage my home. I have often wondered how different that experience would have been had I been at home, alone, as they pulled into my driveway.

As Merita, Wayne, and I met Billy for an evening of dinner and dancing, I completely forgot about the unfamiliar vehicle. I was glad I had changed my mind about going out, or rather, had my mind changed for me. We all rode to Macon together, but Billy was the perfect gentleman and insisted on taking me back to my house at the end of the evening. As we reached Roberta en route to Reynolds, Wayne and Merita took the short cut to my house while Billy and I took the longer route, arriving maybe five or so minutes later.

Wayne's car was already parked in the driveway with the lights off, so I assumed they were inside the house. Parking his car behind Wayne's, Billy and I proceeded towards the house. We were already under the carport before I realized two masked men were standing behind Wayne and Merita with snub-nosed pistols pointing towards their heads. My first impulse was to turn and run, but then I heard Merita's trembling voice, filled with terror: "Willie, please don't run."

The next thing I remember was being at the carport door, gun at my back, with the burglars demanding I unlock the door. I made my way through the house, with the burglar's pistol still on me as I turned on lights in each room. One man forced Merita, Wayne, and Billy into the den to lie face down on the floor, and the other man forced me to go with him down the hall to the bathroom and open a safe I had hidden in the linen closet. I never could determine how they knew of the safe. I was careful not to discuss its existence with others. This man thought I had a good deal of cash in the safe. In reality, there was only about six-hundred dollars in silver half dollars I had been collecting.

Once he removed the coins from the safe, he forcefully led me to the den, instructing me to lie down with the others on the vinyl floor. Merita later dubbed the two masked intruders as the good robber and the mean robber, which is how we still refer to them. Now in the presence of my friends, the mean robber gruffly demanded to know where the money was hidden. When I told him he had it all, he turned to his accomplice and asked sharply, "She wouldn't lie, would she?" as more of a statement than a question. The partner in crime said no, and the mean robber said, "We'll find out. I'll stick a hot cigarette to her. She'll tell us anything we want to know."

"Now remember," the good robber said, "we are to hurt no one."

I breathed a sigh of relief.

After a moment, the mean robber asked me if I had any fishing cord. When I told him no, I heard the other one say, "That's okay. We'll just cut the cords from the drapes." Using the drapery cords, they tied our hands and feet together from the back, leaving us face down on the floor. The intruders then proceeded to go through my house taking what items they wanted: my stereo tapes, albums, mixer, blender, toaster, television, and even my clothes. You name it. We could hear them going through each room of the house as they opened drawers, throwing stuff out as they searched for anything that appealed to them. A few seconds after we heard the attic steps being lowered, they were rummaging through things packed in storage. It took months to reorganize the attic after their assault. All of my clothes, with the exception of one lonely blouse still hanging in my closet, were stuffed into the pieces of luggage retrieved from the attic.

I had cooked a ham the day before, and they found it in the refrigerator. They made sandwiches, sitting down to eat and taking a brief break from their burglary. After recuperating a few moments, they continued to rummage through the house. We remained bound on the floor. After a while, we heard a car drive into the front yard. The men asked us if we were expecting anyone, and we told them no. They told us we'd better not be lying to them "or there would be trouble." After no one came inside, we realized the car they heard must have been their own getaway car, pulling into the driveway to begin loading the things they were piling up in the carport.

Fifteen or twenty minutes after the car left, the two robbers decided to leave, and one asked Wayne for his car keys. I guess they wanted to drive Wayne's car because it was the newest. Wayne pleaded, to no avail, for them not to take his car. They did assure him there would be no harm to his vehicle. When the police later found his car, it was less than a tenth of a mile down the road; the doors were open, and the lights were still on. It was obvious they didn't spend a lot of time transferring things from one vehicle to another. I am convinced the car that drove up in the yard was the two-toned green LTD I had seen earlier. In a final act of humiliating cruelty, they tied our feet to our hands while we lay face down on the floor. Talk about uncomfortable! That was very uncomfortable.

At the time of the attack, I had just finished reading the book *Eighty-three Hours 'Til Dawn*, by Barbara Jean Mackle, about her personal experience of being kidnapped and buried alive in December 1968. While we were bound and face down on the floor, I remember thinking over and over again, "I don't care what you take in this house. Take anything you want. Just please leave me here." I was terrified they were going to take me with them when they left and make me open the beauty shop to see if they could find any more money or anything of value.

It was the mean robber who threatened us as they were leaving, stating, "When we leave, don't you tell anybody, or we'll be back." A few minutes after we heard Wayne's car back out of the driveway, Billy rolled and snail-crawled across the floor to the pantry. He told me, "Willie, I may be going to cut your floor, but I'm fixing to break a Coca-Cola bottle to get us free." Keep in mind, he had his hands tied behind him and his feet tied up to his hands. I don't know how he managed it, but he broke that glass bottle without cutting himself or the floor. Within minutes, he had the rest of us cut loose as well. Wayne jumped to the telephone immediately to call his daddy, Uncle Will Parks, who lived next door. Merita hollered at him, "No, no, no! We can't tell anybody! Remember, we can't tell anybody or they'll be back!" The three of us looked at her in disbelief and in perfect unison said, "Shut up! We are calling for help!"

Uncle Will called the sheriff, and the deputy sheriff called the Georgia Bureau of Investigation. It was well after midnight on Friday night, and Merita and I realized we soon had to be at the salon. We were supposed to open at 4:30 a.m. for our regular Saturday-morning customers. Needless to say, we didn't get much sleep. The sheriff and other officers never took fingerprints. I have always believed the police officers thought my ex-husband, Swilling, might be behind this incident, and I have always felt they really didn't want to find the true culprits due to him being the county game warden and from a locally prominent family. I would not allow myself to believe, however, that he could have ever done anything to put our son in harm's way.

I was so grateful Duane was not at home the night of the burglary. Knowing I would not be home from my date until late in the night, I dutifully made arrangements for him to spend the night with one of his friends. The burglars were thoughtless and cruel, even to a little three-year-old boy who wasn't there. Duane had a little dog he absolutely loved, and they were maliciously low in taking this little dog with them when they left. We never saw that little dog again, and I had to explain to my heartbroken son that someone had come along and kidnapped his dog. For a long time, I was concerned that someone would tell him about the burglary, but no one did and it was years before I ever told him. I simply did not want him to be afraid of living in the house where there had been a break-in. I certainly was not afraid to continue living there. After all, I wasn't going anywhere. He was well into his teenage years before I revealed this secret.

As we opened the beauty salon that Saturday morning after the burglary, I explained to Merita that I thought it best not to mention the incident to anyone who came into the salon that morning; we both were well aware of small-town talk and that as soon the sun rose, everybody would know about it anyway. People would be coming in throughout the day, and it would be exhausting telling the story over and over. I thought it would be better to not get started any earlier than necessary. We agreed mum was the word, at least initially. We did, however, take Shelvie into the small kitchenette area and share the horrifying story. She just looked at us and laughed and said, "No way! You don't think I'm going to believe that story, do you?" We showed her the marks and bruises on our hands and wrists where we'd been bound; she was shocked.

Sure enough, we didn't tell anyone else in those early morning hours, but as soon as the sun was in the sky, word spread like a wildfire, and people began coming in to hear the details. We had no sleep that night, either! In fact, after we finished working that day, the four of us—Merita, Wayne, Billy, and I—returned to Macon to dance the night away and work off some frustrations. I suppose a contributing factor in my decision to attempt to manage the story of the burglary were my feelings about gossip. Beauty salons have always been known as gossip places, and I just never liked small-town gossip, or any gossip for that matter. I had a rule in my salon: We can't help what we hear, but we don't have to repeat it!

The identity of the two masked burglars remains a mystery. There was a great deal of speculation throughout the county, with the general idea being that my former husband, Swilling, was responsible in one way or another, but I didn't think that was the case. I had no proof of who was responsible, but I really believed he was not involved. I would lay awake at night and replay the scene over and over again in my mind, trying to identify these men. Merita and I rehashed the incident time and time again. We both knew the voice sounded very familiar, but we couldn't quite put our finger on it. At one time, Merita had dated a man named Don, and we knew one of the voices sounded like his, but we also knew it wasn't Don who had burglarized us.

Gradually, she and I pieced together our own theory. The salon was always closed on Mondays, and, at the time, the only place to shop was in Macon. We would drive to Macon on our day off to shop at Davison's (now Macy's) department store. Davison's provided a private parking lot for its customers. The lot had an attendant; I'll call him Frank. Because of the frequency of our shopping excursions, we were on a first-name basis with him. The next time I saw Merita, I asked her who she thought Frank's voice sounded like. She immediately responded, "Don."

Two or so years after the burglary, I was attending a hair convention in Macon at the Dempsey Hotel. I was walking through the lobby and heard a man's voice call out to me, "Hey, Willie," and immediately I thought, "That voice belongs to one of the guys in my house the night of the burglary." I acknowledged his greeting and tried to move on, casually, about my business.

It took me a few years, and I admit I may be wrong, but I do think I finally know now who was responsible. We discussed the similarities and determined we had nailed it. In our heart of hearts, we knew.

Officer Jerry Morrow

Chapter Five

The Love of My Life

Since the burglary occurred on the first date I had with Billy, most people thought he wouldn't ask me for another date, but he did. I dated Billy for about six months. And then I met the love of my life. One night, I went to the Civilian Club, a place in Warner Robins where we went to dance. I went with my niece Merita and her date, John. When we got there and after we had gotten a table and were sitting down, John, uncharacteristically, asked me to dance first. There were two guys sitting at the table next to us, and one of them was very nice looking. Of course, I had my eye on him. At first, as I learned later, he didn't know which of us two girls was John's date.

After our dance, John took me back to the table and then danced with Merita. It was summertime, and the windows near our table were open. While I sat alone, I happened to look down on the floor, and I saw a big black bug. I looked at the good-looking guy and said, "Would you kill that bug, please?" Realizing then that John was not my date, he jumped up eagerly, got rid of the bug, and asked me to dance.

As we talked while on the dance floor and later sitting at our table, I learned Jerry Morrow was a policeman in Perry; his two young daughters, Terrie and Debbie, lived in Warner Robins with their mother. He, in turn, learned I was a hair stylist in Reynolds with a three-year-old son. We danced and laughed and danced some more, quickly learning enough about one another to know we wanted to see each other again. We thoroughly enjoyed the evening, which ended much too soon for us both.

As we were walking out of the club, he asked me if I'd cut his hair if he came to Reynolds. I responded shyly, "Sure, I'd be glad to."

"Well," he said, "Come next weekend, I'll come to Reynolds, and you can cut my hair. Then I'll take you to Macon for dinner."

That sounded just fine to me, and the next week became the longest week of my life, overflowing with excited anticipation.

A short time after we began seriously dating, I introduced him to Duane, who was almost four by this time. It was love at first sight for both of them. Duane thought the sun and moon rose and set on Jerry Morrow, and he wasn't the only one. Jerry would pick up his girls every other weekend for a visit, and we spent additional time together on holidays. We easily developed a simple but happy routine to our lives, enjoying each new day and experience while we began to build toward our futures together. But life has a way of throwing you curves when you least expect them.

When Jerry and I first met, he told me he had been dating his next-door neighbor. Upon discovering Jerry was dating me, she became quite upset, persuading him under false pretenses to marry her. As I came in from work one evening, I discovered the letter he had left, explaining what had occurred, his obligation and intent to marry her and do the honorable thing. He apologized profusely and emphasized he truly didn't want to hurt me. I was devastated, totally and completely devastated! This came out of the blue, and my world was rocked beyond comprehension. I knew this man was the love of my life, and I was crushed. I cried for days, actually months, grieving for the man I loved and the life we would have shared together.

I'm not sure exactly how much time had passed when he telephoned one night requesting to come over and talk. He was humble and embarrassed as he explained to me his terrible mistake, begging me to forgive him. He had been married to the woman he had been dating before I met him only two or three months, and it was over. As he explained the circumstances regarding the deception and the pending divorce, he pleaded with me to forgive him and take him back. I really loved this man and so did Duane. I knew we would make a good family, even though many people thought I was making a mistake. Thank goodness I forgave him and took him back. We continued to date for a couple of years, falling head over heels in love with one another.

Jerry and I got married July 6, 1973. A Perry policeman couldn't live outside the county he policed, so he had to get another job. Of course, we didn't want to leave Reynolds because I had a house and the beauty salon there. So, he went to work at Bluebird Body Company in Fort Valley. Bluebird makes school buses, and Jerry' job was in the steel warehouse loading and unloading the steel as it was delivered via Southern Railroad. The conductor's name was Hubert Humphrey; he and Jerry became good friends.

Jerry, lookin' good

Wedding announcement

"Jerry Daddy" and Duane

It turned out that Jerry had always wanted to be a men's hair stylist. So, as it has always been my belief that people ought to pursue their dreams, I encouraged him to enroll at Macon Technical College to become a barber and stylist. "Don't think how long it's going to take," I advised him. "Just take it one day at a time. When you finish, you'll look back and say, 'Where did that time go?'"

He would leave early in the morning to go to Bluebird to his job, and then after he got off work there, he'd leave and go to Macon to the barber college. He'd get home about eleven o'clock at night. Sure enough, once he finished, he looked back and wondered where the time went: "I can't believe it's over," he said. He kept working at Bluebird for a little while, and he'd come to the salon and work on the weekends cutting hair. Soon, though, he left Bluebird and was totally in the beauty salon with us. It was meant to be.

The afternoon of Friday, July 6, 1973 Jerry and I drove to Hawkinsville. I wore a simple Sunday dress and Jerry wore a suit. We did not want a lot of hoopla or frills. We just wanted to get the job done. Through the gentle guidance of our friend, we dedicated our lives to one another and lovingly spoke our vows before God. Our former pastor officiated as he pronounced us man and wife, and I became Mrs. Jerry Morrow. We then drove to Callaway Gardens to spend our first weekend together as husband and wife. Duane spent the weekend with his best friend, Derek Brunson. They attended school together and Patsy, Derek's mother, always kept Duane whenever I was out of town. The girls at the Beauty Nook had written this statement across the mirror at my station, for all to read as they came into the salon that weekend: Jerry & Willie have gone to get married, July 6, 1973.

We made a great family. Duane called Jerry "Daddy Jerry." It was Duane's idea to call him that. He just announced his plan one day; "Mama, I'm going to call Jerry 'Daddy.' I'll call him 'Daddy Jerry.'" They played board games together and would spend hours doing so, with checkers being one of their favorites. Duane was more of a hunter than Jerry, but, oh, how they loved to fish together! Jerry never missed a game when Duane was playing, regardless of whether it was football, basketball, or baseball. In addition, playing golf grew to be one of their special times together.

Now, Duane did see his birth father some. Duane would go to visit when his birth father would come to pick him up, but he got to where he didn't want to go, and I just always told him, "When you get to where you look at him and say 'I don't want to go,' then you don't have to go, but I'm not going to say you can't go because they'll blame me for it."

I'll never forget the day that Duane looked at him and said, "I don't want to go." He must have been, probably, about ten. Then it wasn't long before Duane started wanting to have his last name changed. I told him that when he got grown, we'd change his name if he wanted to. I was afraid if I went ahead and changed his name at that time, while he was still so young, he might resent it when he was older. I knew that children can sometimes be very indecisive and don't really know what they want while they are young. He never wavered.

When he grew up, he still wanted his name changed, so I had it changed for him. It was when Duane started to work after he got out of high school that he brought it up again. He was working at Primerica, which was A. L. Williams then, and he said, "Mama, nobody knows I'm your son. I want my name changed so that everybody knows I'm your son."

So I said proudly, "Okay, we'll have it changed." What's a mama to say after that? And we did. We kept his last name and made it his middle name, out of respect for his grandparents. So his name is Duane McElmurray Morrow. The grandparents were pleased, but they also loved Jerry and the daddy he had become to their only grandson.

Chapter Six

We Don't Say "I Can't"

I love children and always have. When I talk to them, I like to get down on their level. I even get on my knees so I can look them in the eye. Mothers used to come into the beauty salon all the time talking about their children being disrespectful or mean. I would tell these mothers, "If you tell your children they are mean, they are going to think that is the way they are supposed to be. If you tell them how sweet they are, and what a good child they are, that will reinforce the positive." In other words, put those positive ideas in their little minds. If you say those negative things, they are going to think Mama expects them to be mean. Isn't that just common sense? Duane was no exception. Positive input produces positive output.

When Duane was just a small child, I introduced the now famous no-no chair into our home. This popular, small, straight-backed chair, designed specifically for children, was low to the ground and painted bright red with a straw seat. Once Duane could sit on his own, when he would misbehave or was disobedient, he would have to sit in the no-no chair, with stern instructions not to get up from that chair until I told him he could. Surprisingly, unlike most children that age, he never tried to get up before I told him he could. I still have that little chair to this day. Only now, I use it as a book rack in the half bath next to my kitchen at home.

Duane was a very easy child to manage and raise. I soon realized communication and voiced expectations were key elements for him. If we were attending a function together and I explained to him prior to our arrival how I expected him to act, he had no problem. However, if I forgot to explain to him my expectations, he was more likely to misbehave because he did not know his boundaries or my expectations.

As he grew older and needed to be disciplined, I discovered that if I took favorite things such as his go-cart and or his three-wheeler away from him, he heard my message much more clearly. I would always take them away long enough that it hurt: at least a month. He would have to mark off the calendar day by day for all thirty days. Some parents become lenient and rescind their decisions after a week or so, but not me. If I said thirty days, it was thirty days, and I made it a point to never waver in my disciplinary decisions. The message was heard, and it paid off, too.

Raising Duane was an adventure in parenting not just for me, but also for our nanny, Rubye. Rubye Johnson was recommended to me by one of my customers at the beauty salon when Duane was just a toddler. Almost immediately, she became a mainstay in our home, our hearts, and our lives. Beyond a shadow of a doubt, she is the greatest nanny God ever put on the face of this earth! I thank goodness He placed her in Reynolds, Georgia. She was a pleasure from the day we met and remains family to this day. Cars were not equipped with car seats at that time, and as we drove each morning to pick her up, Duane would begin jumping on the seat with excited delight when he saw her. She could hardly get seated in the car before he would grab her around the neck and give her a big hug and kiss. She was not as strict as I, but for the most part, she followed my rules with him. I certainly had no complaints. She was a fabulous cook, having that natural talent and ability to make it look easy. I could tell her in the morning I was going to have guests for dinner, and by the time I arrived in the evening, she would have a dinner table of food prepared that looked like something displayed in a magazine.

She was there through the divorce, the burglary, and, of course, Jerry. After the burglary, Rubye lived with Duane and me for a long while. Duane loved Rubye and always told her when he married and began a family she would have to help raise his children. When that time came, he went by her house in Reynolds and asked her if she was ready to move to Atlanta. She said yes, and she grinned from ear to ear. She packed up and followed Duane and his growing family to Lawrenceville, Georgia, then to New Jersey, California, and back to Atlanta. She was able to remain with Duane and his family until after his third child was born. She then began to develop back and knee problems and returned to Reynolds. All who know her will readily agree that her name fits her well. She is a true jewel.

Duane probably got fewer spankings than most children did because he knew he didn't want one of my spankings. Well, I say that to be funny; he was really a very easy child to manage, and he did seem to respect what I said to him, especially things about his future. For example, as he was growing up, I always told him that he shouldn't get married before he was at least twenty-five and that he needed to work and save at least $100,000 before he married. That advice, of course, was so that he wouldn't start off upside-down like most people do. And he listened to my advice. When he married, he was almost twenty-six and had saved $100,000—or more!

Believing as I always have and teaching him, too, that "I can do all things through Christ that strengthens me" and being positive, I think, has a lot to do with the way we live our lives. I guess to him, those beliefs make a lot of sense, just as they do to me.

From the time Duane began the first grade, I would take him with me to the beauty salon in the morning. He would putter around and play, like small children do, while waiting for the school bus to pick him up and transport him to Beechwood, a private school in Marshallville. The year he completed the ninth grade, the school closed, and he attended Taylor County High school his tenth grade year. We moved to Norcross, Georgia, that summer, and he graduated from Norcross High School. He was always a good student, and studying came easy for him. He also had a dual incentive; he knew he had to have good grades to be allowed to play sports by the school's requirements and more importantly, his mama's requirements.

As the school bus stopped outside the beauty salon each afternoon, Duane would bounce off the bus and play outside for hours. I could watch him and work at the same time. Occasionally, he would come inside to ask me if he could do this or that, and I had taught him if I said no, he was to say, "Yes, Mama" and go back outside. I explained to him I expected him to be polite and obedient. He knew better than to stand beside my chair and beg or whine. If I told him no, I had a good reason for saying no, and as soon as I finished with my customer, I would explain to him my reason. He was very good at obeying this rule, and my customers were amazed. I also taught him to be nice to people, respect adults, and speak courteously and with manners. Frequently, when he would come into the salon, he would speak to each of the adult ladies personally, often hugging their necks, much to their delight

Merita's son Kenny was the same age as Duane. When they were about ten, Scotty, a little boy who lived across the street from the beauty salon, was teasing them as they played outside. Having had his fill of Scotty's shenanigans, Duane picked up a dirt clod, threw it full force into Scotty's face, and knocked him off his bike. Blood from his split lip gushed everywhere. When I realized what had happened, I made Duane go over to Scotty's house, ring the doorbell, tell Scotty's mother, Cheryl, what had happened, and apologize. This was far more torturous to Duane than if I had whipped him. Later, Cheryl told me this was the best punishment I could have given him for the incident. He was embarrassed and humiliated every minute of standing and talking with her. He never got into another fight that I knew about.

One day, when Duane was about seven, he and Mia (my godchild) were playing under the carport when they had a brainstorm. They found a hubcap and poured gas into it and then took a battery charger and sparked it over the gas, producing a cloud of thick, black smoke that billowed from the carport. His timing is always perfect! Jesse McDowell, another great nanny who would fill in for Rubye sometimes, just happened to be coming out of the house and witnessed this frightening sight. A quick thinker, she immediately put out the fire and administered some well-deserved punishment to both children. I always wondered how Duane knew the battery charger would ignite the gas. Maybe it was one of those fix-it lessons he observed.

The pond on the left side of our house was forbidden territory, and Duane knew he was never to go near the pond unless an adult was with him. One time, when Duane and Kenny were playing together in the back yard, Kenny took off running towards the pond. Knowing the danger that lay ahead, Duane took off after him in an attempt to stop him. The eagle eye of Rubye spotted the boys as they were running full speed ahead, and she took off running after them herself. Recognizing she would never catch them before they reached the pond, she screamed "Stop!" and both boys stopped dead in their tracks. When she caught up with them, whether from fright or anger, or maybe a little of both, she was spanking them both as the three breathless runners returned to the house. Back then, it seemed as though whenever Kenny and Duane were together, there was mischief of some sort lurking nearby.

Every summer, First Baptist Church held a vacation Bible school as a treat for all of the local children. Mia, being a few years older than Duane, was in a different class, and this particular day, Duane decided he wanted to attend Mia's class. She tried to explain he had his own class and even the teacher, Mrs. Walton, attempted to reason with him. He was having none of it. He wanted to be in the same class with Mia. Mrs. Walton finally called me at the salon and explained the situation. After excusing myself from my customer, it only took me a few moments to arrive at the church. I took Duane by the hand as we walked outside; kneeling on the sidewalk, I got down to his level so I could look him in the eye, telling him in no uncertain terms he was misbehaving. I wanted him to go back into the Bible school, go into his class, and act like the little man I knew him to be and to straighten up. Mrs. Walton called me that evening and told me she didn't know what I had told Duane, but she wished some of the other mothers would learn from me and tell their children the same thing and mean it. An incident such as this never again happened.

Jeffrey Scott, Kevin Wilder, and Duane have always been close friends growing up and as young boys do, they were never short of their own degree of mischief. At about sixteen or so, Duane's paternal grandmother, Mattie Emma, gave him an older model Toyota Land Cruiser. I was not in favor of a sixteen year old having a vehicle, but she had given it to him. He loved that car! I could not believe it.

One cold December day, Jeffrey, Kevin, and Duane were driving the vehicle in and out of the river swamp behind Uncle Will's house and ours. They were having the time of their lives until they discovered that Land Cruisers were never designed to go through five feet of water. So, there they were, stuck in the deep, muddy water of the river swamp. They literally had to wade out of the swamp, in the dark and without a flashlight to light their way home. When they arrived, they were soaking wet from the swamp water. They told Jerry what had happened, and he called Ricky Eubanks to help pull the Land Cruiser out of the swamp. "A mess" does not even begin to describe the scene; it took some serious doing to get that Land Cruiser cleaned up and operational again. To this day, both Jeffrey and Duane still laugh about their adventure.

❧

"If you clean toilets, make sure you are the best toilet cleaner in existence," I would instruct Duane. He was taught from the time he was a toddler to do his best, no matter what he was doing. He took that advice to heart, and even as a very young child, he always wanted to do things right and to please people.

After we moved to Norcross, Duane worked part-time after school at the Crowne Gas Station near our home. I stopped one day to fill the car with gas, and Charles, the manager, began praising Duane's work ethic profusely, and said, "Mrs. Morrow, I don't know what you did to that boy as he was growing up, but he's the best employee I have ever had in all the years I've been in business."

In response, I said, "I just taught him right, taught him to do his best no matter what he did, that even if he was clean-ing toilets, he should make sure he cleaned them the best anyone could possibly do."

I instilled in Duane that if he was good to me and did what I asked of him, I, in turn, would be good to him and allow him to do some of the things he wanted to do. I con-

The "no-no chair"

Duane and his garden

"Uncle" Will Parks

Duane's love, Kim

Rubye Johnson and Duane's firstborn, Ramey

stantly told him he could be and do anything and do it better than most. We never used the words "I can't" or "I'll try." We did believe in three words: "Always be positive." I've always believed and practiced with him that for every problem, there is a solution. There's a way over it, under it, around it, or through it.

At nineteen, Duane went to work for A. L. Williams, beginning as a retirement-planning clerk for Common Sense Trust, a new fund company they were just starting. He eventually worked his way up the proverbial corporate ladder to executive vice-president of marketing. I've always been proud of Duane and his many accomplishments, but even more, this mama is proud of the man he has become. I just wish every mama could know the joy of having a son as special as he has always been, and I never miss an opportunity to tell him. Even when he started to work as a teenager, I would go by his workplace and leave a note of encouragement on his car from time to time as a simple reminder.

৶

One of the many qualities I admire in my son is his unique willingness to listen to advice and wisdom, consider the source, and then apply that advice or wisdom and principles to his own life. As I said, I suggested he should wait to marry until he was at least twenty-five; to be able to work and save at least $100,000. He was almost twenty-six when he married and had saved more than I had recommended. The Biblical principle of "I can do all things through Christ which strengtheneth me," along with positive thinking, have given us a solid foundation.

The Kendrick family lived about two miles down the road from our house in Reynolds. They had three children: Kim, a few years younger than Duane, her younger sister, Maria, and their baby brother, Jeremy. Their father, Lesley, worked for Goodroe Appliance for many years. When Mr. Goodroe passed away, Lesley bought the appliance store and continues to own and operate it. His wife, Sandra, worked for Flint Electric Membership Corp. Our families knew each other well. We were neighbors and friends, even attending the same church.

As the end of Kim's senior year of high school approached, she, like most young girls, began preparing for her senior prom. She had shopped for the perfect dress, shoes, and accessories, all of which were in her bedroom, waiting for the right moment. Kim had recently broken up with her boyfriend, and the young man she had just started dating was already committed to attending the prom with one of her friends. With no date, she made the decision to go alone to the prom or take her younger brother. Fortunately, her parents would not hear of either plan and told her to invite someone. They even went so far as to suggest two young men they knew, Jonathan Philpot and Duane Morrow.

Our family had moved from Reynolds several years before this time, and contact between our families was no longer frequent. Before the prom, Duane had returned to Reynolds to attend a function at the high school and to visit old friends. As the story is told, Kim saw him at that school function and asked him if he would take her to the prom. Of course, he said yes, and that is how their story began. They never looked back, keeping their eyes totally focused on their future together.

Kim wanted to finish college before she married, and Duane had goals of his own. She majored in speech pathology, graduating from Georgia State University after attending Brewton Parker College in Mt. Vernon, Georgia, for two years. They made it happen! Strangely enough, when they did marry and were en route to the Virgin Islands for their honeymoon, of all the people to run into, they saw Jonathan Philpot, the other young man Kim's parents had suggested as a prom date. He and his new bride were on their way to the same resort and to a room only four doors from the room reserved for Duane and Kim. They had married on the same day as Duane and Kim.

Duane and Kim now have five remarkable children and an incredibly beautiful life together. He could not have a more perfect wife. She has been right there for him, supporting him all the way. As his career has developed and the travel responsibilities increased, she has traveled with him at every available opportunity. As he has received promotions and needed to relocate, she has never batted an eye. She has risen to the occasion, brushed herself off, rolled up her sleeves, and started packing again to make a home in their newest location. They were in New York a few years, then California, London, and Spain. To date, they have moved seventeen times and lived in eighteen houses. What a job she has, and her ability to manage it is phenomenal. While they were liv-

ing in London, Jerry and I visited them a few times. I liked
England. I believe I could live there.

Duane and Kim Morrow

Chapter Seven

The Girls

When Jerry and his first wife divorced in the late '60s, their daughters, Terrie and Debbie, remained in Warner Robins with their mother. As we began to date, the girls were, of course, part of our lives, and we worked hard to blend our families. We would drive to Warner Robins and pick them up for weekend visits, vacations, and special occasions. Terrie and Debbie were in high school when our world suddenly and dramatically changed: they came to live with us in Reynolds. Our established routines and relatively quiet household immediately took on a completely different atmosphere. Duane now had two full-time sisters, and these two sisters now had a full-time little brother. As teenagers, the girls were already pretty much set in their ways, and their ways were very different from how Duane was being raised.

For starters, I had encouraged Duane to eat a variety of foods, with a strong focus on green vegetables, and he went along with it, except for those marshmallows! He absolutely loved them, and I imagine by the time he was an adult, he probably had eaten a submarine full of them. He was not a big candy eater in general. Terrie and Debbie, on the other hand, were extremely picky about any food they ate, disliked most green vegetables, and healthy eating of any kind. Their foods of choice were hamburgers, French fries, and creamed potatoes.

Jerry believed the multiple adjustments Terrie and Debbie were having to make regarding their move were overwhelming; he did not want to alienate his girls by being too strict or demanding, especially about "unimportant things." So, Jerry was not as strong a disciplinarian as I was when it came to eating habits and food selections. The side effect of this was that Duane also became somewhat picky about the foods he would eat. I could not require him to eat certain foods if his sisters did not have to eat them as well. There were other adjustments on all our parts and at times, as anyone who has ever had a teenager knows, things did get a little rocky, but we managed. Schedules had to be rearranged, different accommodations were necessary, and new rules were implemented. I learned quickly to choose battles carefully.

I believe if you live in a home, you help with the chores around the house, as my mother taught me. The girls were not used to this new rule. Like most teenage girls, keeping their room picked up and clean was not a priority. We had numerous discussions regarding the importance of cleanliness and orderliness. While living with their mother, they had been involved with the various youth activities sponsored by their local church. The girls, together with their mother, were devout Christians and accustomed to attending church and Sunday school each week. Preparing a family of five instead of a family of three to attend Sunday services was a breeze compared to some of the other adjustments we all faced.

To earn spending money during the summers, after school, and on weekends, Terrie and Debbie worked at the salon as shampoo girls, earning tips from the customers for their services. In the beginning this was a struggle, another adjustment. Today, however, both girls talk about how much they learned while living in our home.

One of the definite advantages of living in Central Georgia is having access to fresh farm-grown vegetables and fruits from season to season. For a couple of summers, Duane, Terrie and Debbie worked at the local packing shed as the delicious Georgia peaches came into season. On payday, which was always Friday afternoon, they would hit the door of the salon, wanting Jerry to take them to the mall in Macon so they could spend their hard-earned money. Jerry, being the proverbial teaser and never missing an opportunity, would pretend he had too much to do to clean up the salon in preparation for the Saturday customers. Then they would pitch in and have it looking spiffy in no time. He would continue to joke with them, telling them he had no gas in the car. Sure enough, they would step up to the plate and fill the tank with gas. Oh, yes, and as they were traveling, he became unexpectedly hungry, too. Stopping on the way to eat, the three siblings would pick up his dinner tab. Good, responsible kids!

On one occasion, Debbie came to us, wanting to have some friends over on a Friday night, a few boys and a few girls. They were all polite and well-mannered as they mingled. They listened to music, ate snacks, and played games, just having good, clean fun. Around nine o'clock, believing the group was settled, I excused myself to go to my room and relax a while. An hour or so later, I decided to look in on them. When I started down the hall, I met Duane and his friend Jeffrey. My maternal instincts went into high alert as I recognized there was something just not right! Duane told me the records were falling out of the chair. There were no records falling out of the chair as there were no records *in* the chair. It did not take me long to realize the guys had spiked the punch, and Duane and Jeffrey had had their fill. Initially, like teenagers do, they all denied knowing anything about the spiked punch. I was not to be fooled, and the girls were in trouble for allowing the boys to spike the punch and for not coming to me and telling me what was happening.

As Saturday morning dawned, it brought a beautiful sunny day, and I had plans for the group. The girls who had attended her party spent the night with Debbie. Knowing they needed to be punished, but also realizing I had to be careful in administering punishment, I woke them early, feeding them a quick breakfast and marching them outside to prune all of the red-tip shrubbery in our yard by hand. There were one hundred plants. While they griped and grumbled amongst themselves, believing I was being unreasonable, they each knew better than to complain to me. I was steadfast in my determination. These days, they still talk and laugh about the lesson they learned as a result of pruning the red tips. I don't think you could get one of them to have red tips in her yard.

When Terrie graduated from high school, she elected to move back to Warner Robins and live with her grandmother. Jerry and I, as a unified front, had explained she could not sit around in Reynolds and expect us to continue to support her. She told us there was nothing to do and nowhere she could find a job in Reynolds. To her shock, we suggested she return to Warner Robins and find a job on the air force base, which she did. She has done quite well for herself, having now logged over twenty-five years of service in building her career. Within a few years of returning and settling in Warner Robins, she met and married Don Roundtree. It was not long before their family began. Kenny arrived first, followed by his sister, Heather. They are both sweet children, and, of course, we welcomed them with open arms into our ever-growing clan. Terrie and Don were divorced after twelve years together, ending their union on amicable terms and keeping their focus on the children.

Terrie has always been outgoing, never meeting a stranger, whereas Debbie is the quiet and reserved soul. Terrie is also the sports enthusiast, often telling us not to ask her to do anything during football season. She is fanatical about following her teams. She was the photographer for her team and followed them everywhere.

As of the writing of this book, Terrie has been dating a fine man, and they are now discussing marriage. She met him through her mother and stepfather, as he is her stepfather's son. The last time I met Duane in town for our regular Thursday lunch, I shared Terrie's plans with him. Duane was surprised she had not called him personally to share her news. Laughingly, he said to me, "I'll fix her; you just watch!" Returning to his office, he called her, spent a few minutes catching up and then told her he had heard through the grapevine of her future plans. She apologized for not calling to tell him the good news, and he laughingly razzed her and said, "Now, let me get this straight. He's your stepbrother and you are dating him, but I'm your stepbrother and you've never asked me for a single date." They both burst into laughter.

Debbie is a full-time, stay-at-home mom, and an excellent one at that. She and her husband, Larry, are the proud parents of two boys, Jerry and Tyler. Both of these young men are just good, well-rounded teenagers and a delight to be around. They have bright futures ahead of them. Jerry and Tyler love to come down to Duane's farm in Reynolds to fish and are pretty good at it, too. We have all learned to give and take in our ever-evolving relationships, but with time, persistence, maturity, and respect we have learned to appreciate and love one another. We are family.

Mike Perry with Jerry and me

Chapter Eight

A Better Way

Being the ever-progressive entrepreneur and always interested in making a better life, I opened a gift shop next to my beauty salon. Unfortunately, my timing was off. The Macon Mall opened not long afterward, and my gift shop suffered. People buy on impulse, and when they shopped in the new mall, they would buy their gifts there as well. The gift shop just wasn't profitable, so it was decision time. I closed the shop and began to keep my eyes and ears open for a new challenge. I was always looking for an opportunity to make more income, and with my attitude, aptitude, and goals, I wasn't going anywhere but upward and onward on the road to success!

The Goddard family in Reynolds owned the funeral home. Goddard's Grocery Store, one of only two grocery stores in Reynolds, was also owned and operated by Mr. George Goddard. Everyone called him "Mr. George." As his son, Ed, came along, he worked side by side in the grocery store with his father, Mr. George. Three generations later, Ed's sons, Mac and Bruce, also followed the family business line in the grocery industry. (Bruce is married to my cousin Kathy, Ralph and Irene's second daughter.) Ed, Mac, and Bruce decided they were going to build a new building and move the grocery store to the new location. That was progress; Reynolds was growing.

The three Goddard men approached me about building a new building next to their new building, so I could expand the salon. I always liked a challenge, so when they suggested the idea of a new building, I thought it sounded good. Jerry and I discussed this suggestion together, as we were in business together by this time. We applied for a Small Business Administration loan of ninety percent of the total cost. Reynolds Industrial Development loaned us the balance.

What a beautiful facility! We were extremely proud and excited the day of our joint grand opening. There were two separate entrances, Jerry's Golden Shears on one side and the Beauty Nook on the other, with an interior door connecting the two salons. The Beauty Nook had ten hair dryers, six stylist stations, three shampoo stations, a kitchenette, and a laundry area, together with a facial room. Jerry's side, catering to the male clientele, had two stylist stations and two shampoo stations.

※

I always maintained a keen eye on the future and tried to be on top of my game, continually pursuing ongoing education. Now, I decided to focus my attention toward an appointment to the Georgia Hair Fashion Committee. This prestigious appointment is the highest honor a stylist can achieve in the state of Georgia. After almost twenty years of professional experience as a stylist, I decided to take the plunge and began studying to pass the exam required to qualify for this appointment. Working long hours with children at home and dealing with life in general made finding time to study for the exam a real challenge, indeed. But I was determined. On January 28, 1978, seventeen nervous candidates showed up for the exam, which was held in Atlanta. Only five of us were successful in our efforts. My persistence paid off, and I breathed a huge sigh of relief when I learned I was one of the five. Congratulations poured in from friends, clients, and family when an article appeared in the *Taylor County News* on February 23, 1978, announcing my appointment to this professional industry committee.

With this appointment, the doors to new and exciting opportunities began to swing wide open, and I loved every minute of it. There were numerous requests from around the state from affiliates of the Georgia Hair Dressers Association to appear as a guest speaker and/or platform worker demonstrating techniques and educating licensed hair stylists on trends in hair styles. It was an exciting time.

⁊⬤

But even more change was coming. One sunny day in 1979, I looked out the window and saw a nice looking man go into Jerry's salon. When he left, Jerry said the man was a guy he met while working at the steel warehouse at Bluebird. This guy, Hubert Humphrey, worked for the railroad in Macon and offloaded steel at Bluebird. Jerry said he wanted to talk to us about insurance. With that new building, I was in debt up to my eyeballs, and, thinking that he just wanted to sell us something, I said I wasn't interested.

A few weeks later, when I saw him walking into Jerry's

salon again, I decided I would be nice and go over to meet him while Jerry was cutting his hair. After introductions, I stood and talked with Hubert and Jerry. Hubert never said another word about insurance. More importantly, he never said a word about saving me any money, a major point of interest for me due to our enormous amount of debt. I had no idea there were different types of insurance with different price tags, nor did I understand the basic principles of how money could multiply and grow for us.

I did not know I could have substantially more insurance protection for less than I was paying for the little coverage currently in place, and I certainly did not understand I could have taken the difference in what I was currently paying and what I could be paying to invest for our future. If he had mentioned saving money, I would have said, "Can you tell me about it before you leave today?" But not a word! He left after his hair was cut, when Jerry told him again we were not interested.

Then, in September 1979, Mike Perry walked into my salon and said, "Willie, I'm going home with you and Jerry. I've got something to show you."

"Okay," I said. I wasn't going to tell Mike he couldn't go home with us. He'd been to our house many times. He dated my niece Merita at one point, and I had dated a friend of his. So home with us he went, after we closed the salon. Sitting at my kitchen table, Mike began to talk to us about his new work, speaking with an enthusiasm I had never before seen in him. I was ready to listen. "Willie," he said, "I'm here to tell you, I found something better for me, just like you always told me I would, and I've found something better for you and Jerry, too." He went on to tell us he was now working with A. L. Williams. Once he explained to us what he was doing, I instantly realized something about my previous dealings with the insurance industry. I had been sold everything but the right thing! I immediately became his client, converting all of my whole-life policies (fourteen of them) into one term-life insurance policy; by doing so, I saved hundreds of dollars. It was not necessary for me to have the I.Q. of an Einstein to understand that two plus two is four. Mike, however, was not content with me only becoming his client. "Willie," he continued, "you need to work with me."

I didn't know whether to laugh, cry, or slap him! "Mike," I said, "you know I don't have the time. I work ten, twelve, sometimes fourteen hours a day at the beauty shop." I declined. He was relentless, though. In a few weeks, he called again, and I declined again. Then, on Christmas Eve Day, 1979, just a few months later, my world as I knew it was rocked, and unbeknownst to me at the time, my entire life was about to change. Only this time, I was going somewhere. I just didn't know it yet.

☙

On Christmas Eve, I was getting dressed to go to Macon with my nephew Edward to buy his wife a Christmas present. All of a sudden, I had a terrible pain in my back and legs. Jerry and Duane had gone to town to eat breakfast at the Deal-a-Burger. The pain was so bad that I called and told Jerry about it, but I told him I thought it would go away. I continued on my shopping trip with Ed, even though I could hardly walk through the mall. When we got home, Ed took me to the hospital in town. There Dr. Whatley examined me and thought I'd probably pulled a muscle, so he treated me for that.

Throughout Christmas Day and the following week, the pain did nothing but intensify at an alarming rate. On New Year's Day, 1980, all I could do was lay writhing in indescribable pain on the floor. The next day Dr. Whatley sent me to the hospital in Macon for an MRI. The shocking diagnosis was that the lower two discs in my back had ruptured. Standing on my feet as a hair stylist over so many years had finally taken its toll. My day of reckoning had arrived. The specialist informed me the discs needed to be fused, and without immediate surgery the possibility of additional discs rupturing and eventual paralysis was a grave reality.

The team of medical advisors described how bone grafts would be taken from my hip for use in the procedure. I would be required to lie flat on my back for a minimum of two months without so much as raising my head above the pillow. I would not be allowed to enter the salon to work for a minimum of six months. I can do all things through Christ who strengthens me, I reminded myself.
"If that is what I need to do, let's get it over with and behind me," I announced to the doctors. With that decision, they began the necessary preparation for surgery without allowing me to go home, even for a few hours. The next day a successful operation was completed, and it was now up to me to allow my body to heal itself. Belinda and Ed were both gen-

erous and kind in inviting the three of us to stay with them through my first two months of recuperation. Belinda was a phenomenal nurse. She missed her life's calling!

While I was still at Belinda's house, Mike Perry came to visit me again. Sitting on the side of my bed, he said, with obvious concern, "Willie, you need to listen to me. I've had the same surgery, and I know from personal experience you are not going to be able to stand on your feet as a hair stylist enduring those long and torturous hours anymore." The more we continued to discuss my future and the business opportunity he was offering, the more interested I became.

"Okay, Mike," I answered, "I realize I need to do something else. Let me get out of this bed and mobile again. When I do, I'll call you and take a serious look at what you are offering." He agreed. No one in the entire world knows how many times I stood behind that salon chair and asked, prayed, and begged God to show me a better way. I loved hairdressing. Never once had I dreaded going to work, but I was killing myself, and I knew it. Then again, I didn't know where I could go to make the kind of money I was making. Number One: I was a woman. It was the '70s, remember? Number Two: I had no college degree. Number Three: I was in a small Central Georgia town. And Number Four: I was a blonde! Just where do you think I could go?

I knew I would be in bed for months, followed by additional months of healing and therapy as I began the journey of rebuilding both my strength and stamina before I could sit down with Mike and seriously consider this opportunity. Never being one to sit still—I watched little television and definitely no soap operas—I knew I needed to find something to occupy my time while I was confined to the bed. I decided to use my time constructively. I would write a cookbook. Throughout my life, cooking had always been a passion, one that mother had instilled in me as a child. I was constantly exchanging recipes with my customers and friends. I thought publishing a cookbook would be an interesting endeavor and would definitely keep me busy while I recovered from surgery.

One of the unexpected joys I experienced while being basically incapacitated the first two months out of surgery was bonding with Anne, Belinda's nursing assistant. Anne was my two-year-old grandniece, Belinda and Ed's only daughter. As her day began each morning, I could clearly hear her tiny little feet when they hit the floor, racing down the hall as she made a beeline to "Rene's" room to offer her lovable brand of help. (My friends have always called me Willie; my family always called me Rene.) I learned to relish the sound of those precious feet as they would pitter-pat towards my room, bringing the joys, innocence, and excitement of childhood into my day. Each day she was faithful, coming to visit with me and checking on me, offering whatever assistance she could and always bringing her own special recipe for laughter and delight.

In the mornings before he left for work, Jerry would put all of my paperwork and recipes on the bed, setting things up so I would be able to reach whatever I needed during the day. In the evenings, he would lovingly and diligently remove everything so I could get a good night's sleep. Duane was always around and forever willing to offer his flavor of dedicated help as well. I had excellent care through the love, attention, and pampering of all these people. I will always be grateful for the tireless support, prayers, and love I received from near and far through the entire recovery process.

I had contacted Bob and Elaine Cochran, owners of Taylor County Printing Company, to print my book. I carefully copied each recipe by hand, never lifting my head above the pillow. Then someone who worked for the Cochrans would type each one for my review. One of my customers in the salon, Emily Harp, drew the artwork for the cover (a Georgia peach, of course) and another, Catherine Brady (everyone called her "Cat") created the interior art details. As a result of the work, *Southern Favorite Recipes* was created and has continuously been a great seller.

Months later, to my delight, my doctors were impressed and pleased when I presented them with an autographed copy of the cookbook I had written while in bed. So many patients, I learned, would just lay in bed becoming more miserable by the day. I must say, working on my cookbook was a good way to spend the time. Publishing a book was quite a therapeutic endeavor, and fun. Both the *Taylor County News* and the *Macon Telegraph* wrote articles about the cookbook and the circumstances in which it was created.

Each and every recipe contained in *Southern Favorite Recipes* is tried and true. I have personally cooked every recipe included in the publication. Over the years, I have had many people tell me one of the reasons they like the book so well is they know when they pick it up to find a recipe, almost always the necessary ingredients are already in their pantry or refrigerator. I have continued to collect new and interesting recipes in all categories from a number of different friends, family, and various sources. Fans, friends, family, and business associates have, over the years, encouraged me to publish a second edition of the cookbook. In the spring of 2010, *Southern Favorite Recipes, Volume Two*, containing all of the recipes from the first edition and some new recipes, was published. I elected to keep the initial cover artwork by Emily Harp because the peach picture is so reminiscent of my Southern roots. This edition is a hardback and is available through many venues.

When the two months of absolute confinement to bed had passed and I had recovered well enough to be somewhat mobile, I called Mike and told him I was ready to talk. He sat down with me at the kitchen table and explained the A. L. Williams business opportunity. The very next weekend, I attended a seminar as the guest of Mike and Carol Perry; Art Williams himself was the host and speaker. After the first session, Mike asked me what I thought and, without hesitation, I looked him square in the eyes and said, "There's no one, anywhere, except the Good Lord Himself, going to stop me from this opportunity. Just get me trained and get out of my way!"

Chapter Nine

Atlanta or Bust!

The doctors who performed my surgery had emphatically told me I could not return to work at the salon, and I was banned from standing on my feet for a minimum of six months. When the six-month date arrived, I hardly noticed. By then I was fully entrenched in the business opportunity with A. L. Williams. I never picked up another brush or comb professionally. I realized I'd found the answer to my prayers. Be careful what you ask God to provide. You just might get it!

My experience with finding my answer reminds me of the joke about the man who, when the floods came, would not get into the rescue boat. He told the would-be rescuers that God would take care of him. As the flood waters continued to rise, a motorboat crew offered him a ride to safety. Still he would not accept the offer of help, answering, "God will take care of me." As the waters rose to roof height, he became even more alarmed and climbed to the top of his chimney, waiting. Soon a helicopter appeared, having been sent by the rescuers, but again he refused the help, repeating his belief that God would take care of him. He drowned. As he arrived at the pearly gates, he pleaded for understanding with his Maker, and said to God, "I have been faithful to you all of my life. Why didn't you take care of me as you promised?" Then

God responded, "I sent a rowboat, a motorboat, and even a helicopter to help you. What more did you want?"

In my personal version of this story, after having prayed for years for something better, Hubert came to see us twice, and I said no. I continued to pray, asking God to help me find something better, then Mike came along, and again I said no. I kept praying and asking God to show me a better way. He was answering, and I was not listening. Finally, I landed flat on my back—literally—and, finally, He got my attention. I firmly believe that is why I ended up with back surgery: He realized that was the only way He could get my attention.

I will always believe that is why I am where I am today. God sent me a rowboat, a motorboat, and a helicopter. It took continued effort on His part, but finally I said yes. Success, fame, and fortune do not care who owns them. Why not you? I already had a great work ethic, taught to me by my daddy and brothers. I saw them get up every morning and be in the fields planting by four thirty with lights on the tractors. Mother worked hard at her tasks as well, from early morning onward, caring for us and doing all she could to keep our family strong, healthy, and secure. I was prepared for success. I just had to accept what God had ready for me.

The surgery was in January, 1980, and I became active with A. L. Williams the following June. Even though I was no longer present on a daily basis at the Beauty Nook, the other stylists continued on. Jerry was still working on his side of the salon, so there was always the presence of an owner. After attending beauty school in the "big city" of Atlanta, I knew I wanted to live in a larger town. But I never thought it would be possible. I felt trapped, financially. The only thing I was trained to do was style hair, and although I was really good at it, I also knew if I moved, it would take years in a new city to build a clientele large enough for me to be able to make the kind of money I was making in Reynolds.

Once I truly understood the business opportunity offered by A. L. Williams, I was sold hook, line, and sinker (for all you fishermen out there). I knew this was my way out. While Jerry held the proverbial fort down, both at home and at the salon, I went to work building my new business venture and our future.

It wasn't long before I decided I wanted to move to Atlanta. However, I knew we still had the multiple responsibilities associated with the building housing the salons. It took me four years to find the right person to purchase the building, but the timing still wasn't right. After a while, I made an offer which could not be refused, and it was accepted. I did not want that building to keep me from this golden opportunity. I knew we were definitely going somewhere, and we were almost ready!

By this time, Jerry's girls, Terrie and Debbie, now seventeen and fifteen respectively, were living with us. We all sat down as a family and discussed the pros, cons, and sacrifices we would have to make to move to the city. We all agreed it was time to make our move. After finishing her senior year of high school in Reynolds, Terrie moved back to Warner Robins to live with her maternal grandmother, as mentioned previously. While Duane and Debbie hated leaving their friends, I promised them it would not be long before they would both thank me for having the courage to pick up and begin over again.

It did take courage but, remember, I am driven by God's promise of security, "I can do all things through Christ which strengtheneth me," and that promise remains at the forefront of my mind. Our financial security was in Reynolds, where we had a three-bedroom brick home that was completely paid for and two thriving and successful salons. A lot of people thought at the time we were crazy to risk everything we had for an unknown future. I knew that God had answered my years of pleading and helped me. I wasn't about to let Him down.

&.

By January of 1984, I had met many new business associates through my affiliation with A. L. Williams. One such associate, who quickly became a good friend, was Frances Avrett from Sandersville, Georgia. Knowing we both were from small towns, we were acutely aware that our potential success was limited in our individual home locations. We both had a larger vision for our families and our businesses, so our first step in relocating to Atlanta was to move together. Frances and I shared an apartment until June and opened an office in Sandy Springs. After completing the current school year, our children and husbands joined us. Frances and her clan moved to the Roswell area, and we moved to Norcross. Our office was centrally located for both of us, and we continued to build our individual businesses.

After settling into our new home, Duane enrolled in Norcross High School as a junior. He played football and was elected president of the Fellowship of Christian Athletes, as well as captain of the football team. His senior year, he was voted most valuable offensive football player. Debbie graduated from Taylor County High School prior to our move and then started her working career at a Hardee's in the Norcross area. After working there about a year, she began working for McDonalds, where she was promoted to store manager in record time. Not long afterwards, she met a great guy, Larry Booth, who visited the restaurant's drive-through lane almost daily to order his lunch. They began to date and a couple of years later they married. Eventually both Duane and Debbie did thank me for having the courage to move.

Once our move to Norcross was complete, a mutual friend assisted Jerry in securing a job at Davison-Kennedy Railroad in South Atlanta. Jerry worked there a couple of years until another friend offered him a job in construction with Reddick Construction Company, much closer to home. A year or so later, the business moved to Central Georgia. Not wanting to transfer with the company, Jerry applied and was accepted for a job at Primerica, formerly A. L. Williams, in the mail room.

He later moved to the facilities department, working with a terrific group of men and was never happier. This job required physical labor in all areas of the buildings throughout the Primerica complex, so he got to meet multitudes of employees, from the mail room to the upper echelon of management. Jerry quickly made himself known, admired, and loved throughout the company with his unabashed humor and friendliness. He worked for Primerica nineteen years. Having a wife in the field and being an avid Georgia Bulldog fan, he never lacked something to discuss and joke about with his coworkers. Having the history we shared with A. L. Williams/Primerica since 1980, we always thought of ourselves as one of the many proud Primerica families.

Being an agent and in the field, I was able to earn and win many trips sponsored as bonuses by the company. We enjoyed traveling to such luxurious and exotic destinations as Hawaii, the Bahamas, Bermuda, Boca Raton, and Acapulco. These trips were always first class, and the participants were always treated like royalty. We enjoyed a fabulous life, having fun and going everywhere together. Jerry was the completely perfect business partner, because he allowed me to be myself, growing and becoming the fully independent woman I am today. He was my rock!

One of my favorite stories involving Jerry took place on vacation with our friends Mac Goddard and Gene Brunson on St. Simons Island in Georgia. They had invited us to go sailing on this picture-perfect afternoon. Not long after boarding the boat, I realized a prank was in the making, and I watched them carefully. In a few minutes, I saw Mac give Gene the eye and then tip the boat. Before we could brace ourselves or even react, we were all thrown into the Atlantic Ocean. Remember now, I couldn't swim! I grabbed Jerry, holding on to him for dear life and literally climbed on his back, almost drowning him. As I walked onto the beach after having been tossed into the ocean (without so much as a single strand of wet hair) the look of disappointment in the eyes of our hosts was unmistakable. Their sole mission, I later learned, was to flip the boat and to watch as I emerged with my soaking wet hair clinging to my scalp and face. They thought this would be funny and a great laugh as they had never seen my hair wet. It is still a big joke with us today.

Chapter Ten

Jerry

Milan Trammel (known as M. T.) Morrow and his wife, Mary Mildred Munford Morrow, were blessed with the arrival of their fourth child and youngest son, Jerry, on July 20, 1939 in Troy, Ohio. He was a delight straight out of the "chute" as told by those present. Paul and Dick were his older brothers together with his older sister, Judy. Years after his arrival, their baby sister, Carol, joined the family. The family lived in Ohio until Jerry was thirteen, when his family moved to Perry so his father could begin work at the U. S. Air Force base in Warner Robins.

Paul is now the only surviving sibling. He and his wife, Joyce, live in Elizabeth City, North Carolina. Dick, who lived in Ft. Wayne, Indiana, passed away in 2010 from heart disease. Judy Flournoy, who lived in Perry, Georgia, departed in 2005 as a result of ovarian cancer. Upper respiratory disease claimed the life of the youngest sibling, Carol White, in 2002. Several years before I came into the picture, in October of 1970, Jerry lost his father to pancreatic cancer. Shortly after Jerry and I began dating, his mother, Mildred, passed away from cirrhosis of the liver. When her diagnosis was pronounced, no one in the family could understand it; she had never had so much as a sip of any form of alcohol throughout her entire life. It was a painfully sad time in his family. Both of his parents are buried in Perry.

As brief as it was, I will always be grateful I had the opportunity to meet the woman who was to become my mother-in-law. Everyone always said she was such a sweet lady, that is, until you tried to take her picture. I had no idea she hated having her picture taken, but I learned that fact the hard way. Most everyone in the family had gathered at her house one summer afternoon. We were all outdoors preparing for dinner, and as she walked out of the house, I took a picture of her. Man, oh man, the world came to a screeching halt! All of her children instantly froze, and someone muttered quietly, "You're really in for it now." Little did I know! She never missed a beat; she verbally rung me out, up one side and down the other, before she finished her tirade. Believe me; I never dared to take another picture. Her children teased me for years about this incident. No one ever knew why she had such an aversion to having her picture taken. Different strokes for different folks.

During his high school years, Jerry decided he no longer wanted to go to school and withdrew to join the U. S. Navy Reserves. A short time later, he realized his error and the importance of education; only later he did get his G.E.D. He was not in the Navy Reserves long. I believe he was still in boot camp when he was honorably separated due to an injury to his right leg resulting in a lifelong medical condition. While still in high school, he and a friend were driving one night on a dark road when they unexpectedly came upon a tractor driving down the road without lights. The accident happened so quickly that neither driver had time to avoid the crash, which left Jerry with a broken leg. Doctors implanted a steel plate in his leg, which gave him a slight but permanent limp. The strenuous physical training required by the Reserves took its toll on his body as well and ended his desire to serve our country in the armed forces.

Once he left the service and returned to Warner Robins, he went to work at a grocery store, married, and began his family, eventually having his two daughters, Terrie and Debbie. After a few years, he decided he wanted to join the police force. After training, he was inducted into the Perry Police Department and loved it. He worked there as a police officer until we married and he moved to Reynolds.

After I changed careers and went to work with A. L. Williams, Jerry was a total support. He took care of the children when I had to be away from the house for appointments or meetings. My new career had me out in the evenings quite often, and he never complained once about me being gone at night. He was my very best friend. He attended many of the meetings with me whenever possible and so did Duane. Duane enjoyed attending the meetings as well. He liked learning how money worked, not to mention the positive atmosphere that surrounded us. I knew it was a great advantage for him to learn these financial principles at such a young age. I certainly wish someone had taught them to me when I was his age. Like so many others, I did the wrong things with my money simply due to lack of knowledge. There is so much truth in the statement that "What you don't know *will* hurt you."

Jerry loved working with his hands. He shined as he cut and styled his customer's hair. He flourished at refinishing furniture. He was always working on this project or that one around the house and never sat still. Once we moved to Atlanta, he would go to the flea markets and yard sales on weekends; there was no telling what he would find. He just loved to shop. If I said the word "go," he was ready. He would go shopping with me and never once complain. He was an incredible jokester. If he couldn't tell you a joke, he probably didn't have much to say to you.

An instant friendship was born in 1997 when he met a "newcomer" to Primerica, Jim "Buck" Wheat. Jim had recently relocated to Georgia from Michigan and was working in the Office of the General Council. The rapport they shared was both immediate and lasting. Their personalities clicked instantaneously as they joked and teased anyone who would listen. They quickly discovered each had worked as a police officer earlier in their careers. They both loved repairing items and working with their hands. Fishing was an equally fascinating adventure, each having their individual tales to tell about the one that got away. Oh, heavens, let's not forget their sports! Jim once told me that if someone could ever paint a picture of a true good ole boy, it would be Jerry. They simply bonded from the minute they met.

Jim, his wife, Nancy, and Jerry and I socialized on several Primerica sponsored trips until Jim retired in 2006. Our lives became knitted even more closely as Jim began to work in the field as an agent with Primerica, and we saw even more of Nancy. Each Christmas, when Jerry and I hosted a holiday open house, inviting our friends, family, and business associates, Jim and Nancy were always there, helping and supporting.

Jerry and me in Puerto Rico

Judy Bargainnier

The Morrow family, Christmas 2007

&

I knew Jerry for thirty-seven years, thirty-five of those years as a husband. Jerry was definitely the love of my life. Until 2006, I had never known him to be sick other than a minor head cold, and even that was a rarity. That year, he was diagnosed with carpal tunnel syndrome, probably from the constant use of his hands and wrists over the years. The combination of cutting hair, working as a carpenter, and using the tools of his trade on a daily basis took a toll. The surgery went well; he recovered quickly and never missed a beat. Then, in early 2007, he began to mention (he never complained about anything) that he was having difficulty raising his arms to any degree. It wasn't long before he began noticing he was dropping his drill as well as other tools at work.

Through the referral of friends, we made an appointment with a neurologist. After the initial examination, the doctor told us Jerry's condition was one of two things. Either it was a nerve disease which was treatable or it was Lou Gehrig's disease, also known as ALS. Amyotrophic Lateral Sclerosis is a disease of the nerve cells in the brain and spinal cord which control voluntary muscle movement. It is incurable. An appointment was scheduled for further testing.

After the medical tests were run, we scheduled another appointment with the neurologist in February, 2007, to learn the results and hear the doctor's recommendations. We were positive we would hear a good report. Not wanting our children to feel they were excluded, we presented a unified front as a family of five as we settled into the doctor's office. Attempting to keep our positive attitude, we anxiously prepared ourselves for his words.

The news was not good. It was ALS. We were devastated and numb with shock. The doctors looked straight into Jerry's eyes, flatly telling him he had two to five years to live. Like most people in shock, we both heard what we so desperately wanted to hear, the higher number, five. He lived sixteen months from the day he was diagnosed. I am certain the disease had been there long before, and we just missed the signs.

Shock, anger, tears, sadness, and general disbelief overcame us as we quietly walked out of the building that day. We had no idea of the demands the journey would place on us, but we did know we still had hope, faith, and each other. As a family, we knew that we could "do all things through Christ who strengthens us."

Frantically wanting to believe there was a better answer, we went to another physician at Emory University Hospital in Atlanta. He ran his own tests, only to get the same results. We traveled to Johns Hopkins, where a medical professional poured over his records and told us bluntly, "There's no need to do any more tests," and we cried.

When an unexpected experience such as this happens in our lives, we all have a tendency to look back later and wonder how we managed to go through it, but you do. Armed with underlying faith, we individually kept marching forward, praying for a miracle and hoping for the best.

Jerry maintained a positive attitude through it all. He had

incredible caregivers. It was obvious they loved him, as evidenced by the quality of care they gave him, tirelessly. He said, "Well, if this is the hand I've been dealt, then this is what I've been dealt." His caregivers were astonished by his good-natured and positive attitude. He flashed that famous smile of his and continued to tell his jokes.

We were blessed to be able to care for Jerry at home. Primerica markets a variety of financial products and services. When a new product, long-term-care insurance, was introduced in 2002, I immediately bought a policy for us. I believe if I am going to market a product, I'd better own it. Thank goodness God was looking after me in that earlier decision. Our long-term-care plan paid for the excellent care Jerry received throughout his illness. As Jerry's health began to decline, team members from the Comfort Keepers organization were at our home daily. They would stay throughout the day, skillfully administering care and comfort—physical, medical, emotional, spiritual, whatever was needed—for both of us.

Later, the caregivers assigned through Embracing Hospice were present daily, attending to our every need. They were angels! I cannot adequately praise each member of the team or the organizations they represent. The only time Jerry wasn't getting home care was the week he spent in the hospital in May of 2008 after he developed pneumonia. I am convinced this is what actually caused his body in its weakened state to shut down. This was the first and only time I had ever known Jerry Morrow to be hospitalized as an admitted patient.

I had promised Jerry I would be with him through it all. With that vow in mind, I remained at home to be close to Jerry as his condition deteriorated. I went into the office only when absolutely necessary. This was possible because I could set my own schedule as a business owner with Primerica.

Had I known he was going to be taken as soon as he was, I would not have worked a single day. Like most, as I look back, I recognize there were things I did not do which I should have done, things that never occurred to me to do at the time. I literally watched his body turn on him and quit. Day by day, I witnessed as the ravages of this hideous disease caused his body to rebel, eventually stealing his very breath. I knew in my head he was dying, but in my heart, I couldn't or wouldn't allow myself to believe it. I was in total denial.

In the wee hours of the morning of June 19, 2008, as he was sleeping, Jerry simply slipped into the welcoming arms of our Lord, Jesus Christ, healed and instantaneously made complete and whole in the sight of God. I wish God had not taken him so soon or so cruelly. I know he is no longer suffering, and we will see one another again. Although I miss him terribly and life is lonesome without him, I do know that God has a plan. I have faith He is caring for me as I continually grow into the person He has intended and designed me to become.

I have known my good friend Judy Bargainnier since she was a child, as both of us are from the Reynolds area. As an adult, Judy settled in the Atlanta area and eventually joined Primerica as an associate, working through my office. The faithfulness, sensitivity, and compassion of this loyal friend have been invaluable to me over the years. Judy was always at my right side at a moment's notice as Jerry's health began to decline, spending many a night with me through the final weeks of Jerry's life. We were keenly aware of the labored and shallow breathing Jerry was experiencing as we alternated checking on him through the night. Shortly after 3:00 a.m., almost simultaneously, our feet hit the floor running as we made our way to him. The unbelievable had happened. He was gone!

Word of Jerry's passing spread like wildfire through our local church, our neighborhood, the Primerica family, Warner Robins, Perry, and Reynolds. One of the first calls I was able to make was to Duane, who appeared at my door in record time. Fortunately, the night before as he was on his way home from work, he stopped at the house to see his beloved Daddy Jerry for what turned out to be the last time. It was special then, and became even more so as time has moved forward. Frances Avrett, who had experienced the loss her own true love, Lee, a few years earlier, was by my side as daylight dawned, offering comfort, consolation, hugs, prayers, and constant support. Marge Madison, another friend with Primerica, arrived shortly thereafter, bringing her own brand of sympathy and condolences. I have no idea what I would have done without my friends and their support.

❧

Years before, Jerry and I had agreed that we both wanted to be buried in Reynolds. Therefore, it was necessary for the directors of Goddard Funeral Home to drive to our home in Lawrenceville to transport his body and begin making funeral preparations. Hours later, David McLeighton and Willard Wilder arrived. I am filled with humble gratitude to these men for the gentle and compassionate manner in which they worked through the process. I left later that day with Judy at the steering wheel, following Duane and his family as we returned to Reynolds. I was totally numb!

A few days prior to Jerry's passing, several of his coworkers came by the house to visit with him. Among them was Bill Hayden, who brought a gift. As Jerry anxiously waited for me to unwrap the package, we discovered a handsome University of Georgia shirt. Neither of us had ever seen a shirt of this quality and intricate design. It was truly unique, and Jerry was pleased. Bill had no way of knowing he was delivering a heart's desire. Jerry and I had a standing agreement. He wanted to be buried in a UGA shirt, and I wanted to be buried in pink satin pajamas. Over the years, I would periodically remind him he needed to find "his shirt" and have it hanging in the closet, just as I had done. My pink pajamas are hanging in my closet, just in case. He would respond with his wonderful smile and say, "I'm not in a hurry; I've got plenty of time." And as it happened, of course, he didn't! He never found his shirt, but God found it for him, with a special delivery through this sensitive and caring man, Bill. We proudly buried Jerry in his University of Georgia shirt.

I think God knows humans have special needs to be able to function in times of crisis, and He anoints us with a special gift. His merciful gift is numbness. Jerry's funeral was remarkable and completely befitting of the man who loved and was loved by so many. Hundreds upon hundreds paid their respects while visiting the funeral home that hot Friday evening, offering condolences, sharing memories, and honoring his memory. Flowers were everywhere, along with an abundance of donations to the ALS organization in his honor. True to Southern roots and traditional custom, food in the house was overflowing. As is customary in our community of Reynolds, First Baptist Church provided lunch the day of his funeral.

The church was filled to overflowing as Ricky Moyers, a co-worker from Primerica, and Mac Goddard conducted Jerry's service. Terry Robertson, another co-worker, sang "High on the Mountain" and the "I Can Only Imagine" in a voice angels would envy. There were few dry eyes in the church. A spray of brilliant red roses covered the casket. The men with whom he had worked daily in the facilities department, together with several close friends, walked by his side in honor one last time as the official pallbearers. Jerry's coffin was placed in a mausoleum in the Hillcrest cemetery in Reynolds with a space reserved for my body to be next to his when the time comes.

As I remember, there were droves of employees and friends from Primerica who simply could not make the drive to Reynolds for Jerry's funeral. The following day, a Sunday, our family hosted a reception and memorial in the Duluth area, close to Primerica headquarters, to accommodate these friends and associates who also wanted to remember Jerry; this was an equally phenomenal and humbling experience.

Hundreds of corporate employees together with many field representatives and friends came to pay their last respects; the gathering was a blessing for all of us. He was and continues to be dearly loved and respected. As my niece Belinda so clearly stated, "To know Uncle Jerry is to love him," and everyone did!

%

Danny Woodard, who works in the publication department at Primerica, created a gift and delivered it to the Sunday memorial. This beautiful framed collage is almost four feet by two-and-a-half feet and displays pictures collected throughout his life. It hangs on the wall in my office; it is a loving remembrance and tribute to Jerry, the incredible husband, the awesome father, the faithful friend, and the loyal employee. I will cherish it always!

Another special tribute is the poem written by Jerry's good friend, Danny Dunbar, in his memory:

Jerry

He was like a ray of sunshine with that smile upon
    his face.
He was ready to make a new friend any time and
    any place.
He would stop what he was doing just to listen or tell
    a joke,
Anything to make you smile.

Jerry Morrow was just good folk.
He never met a stranger and called everybody friend.
He was the center of attention and was until the end.
His family was his life blood and his "Willie" was
     his heart.
His strength came from God above and each day was
     a brand new start.
He would come back in to visit and it was always
     the event.
He was almost like a rock star,
People would follow where he went.
Heaven is a little brighter and the earth has grown
     more dim,
'Cause he was like a ray of sunshine and the "Light"
     would follow him.
And now he's with the Father, his pain and
     suffering done.
He's in the presence of our Savior, telling jokes
     and having fun.

૪.

Jerry's last Christmas with us was in 2007. On Christmas Day 2007, each member of our entire family dressed in red and met at our home. It was bittersweet, knowing in the depths of our hearts that this could be our last Christmas together. As we all posed for a final family picture, I remember the laughter and fun that enveloped us as we created wonderful memories that linger to this day. This special photo of our family hangs in our home, where I am able to see it on a daily basis and give thanks. The last thing Jerry asked of me before he passed was that I bury a copy of the family picture with him. I did!

I sure do miss him.

Chapter Eleven

Hotel Happiness

Many a morning, as I rise to greet the day, I begin singing the words of the chorus from a song from *Oklahoma* by Rodgers and Hammerstein: "Oh, what a beautiful morning, Oh what a beautiful day. I've got a beautiful feeling, everything's going my way." Also, one of my favorite sayings from Tom Hopkins is "I feel good, I feel fine, I feel this way all the time. I'm alive, I'm awake and I feel great." I believe we should get up in the mornings speaking positive words to ourselves. On one of my birthdays, my girlfriend Camille sent me a wonderful gift of a special little girl bear named Rebecca. She has on a straw hat and is dressed in a denim outfit with the cutest face you could possibly imagine. What makes Rebecca so special (besides being a gift from my dear friend) is she sings the chorus "Oh what a beautiful morning" when you press her paw. I couldn't believe Camille found her. She is awesome, and I love her! Rebecca sits in various places throughout the house, greeting overnight guests with her happy positive song. This song, as I've instructed my family, is to be sung at my funeral someday.

❧

Sandy Carter-Gee and me

My home has always been called "Hotel Happiness." We have had numerous people come and go, many staying with Jerry and me for a while if they needed a temporary roof, regardless of how long "temporary" might be. We loved people and loved having them around, and today I still do. When there was a major event or convention sponsored by Primerica, it was far from unusual to discover our home filled to over-flowing capacity with business associates turned friends.

In May 2000, Sandy Carter-Gee, who was living in Taylor County at the time, joined Primerica through a mutual business associate. Just about the time she completed the requirements to become a fully licensed representative, she and her husband Stanley decided to move to Destin, Florida, where they lived for several years. Prior to moving to Florida, Stanley worked with his son, George, who owns a cabinet shop in Potterville. After moving, Stanley would return to Potterville weekends to work in the shop with his son. The afternoon of October 1, 2007, a friend called to tell me Stanley had passed away suddenly. He was at the cabinet shop and had suffered a massive heart attack. Sandy, who was in Destin, was on her way to Potterville. As soon as I learned the details of the funeral, I told Jerry I felt an urgency to be there for Sandy, and he agreed that I should go. The morning of the funeral, I drove to Butler, Georgia, and after the service, I spent a few private moments with Sandy.

I stayed in touch with her as the weeks passed and turned into months and the months into years. I knew what she was experiencing through her grief; after all, by this time, I, too, had lost the love of my life. Our bond continued to grow even stronger. In one of our conversations, she told me she did not know if she should stay in Florida or move back to Georgia. She had decided, against the advice of her friends and realtor, to put her house on the market. All were telling her it would not sell due to

the market having just taken a nose dive. She went on to say she had put the entire situation in God's hands and would ask Him for help in selling the house if she was meant to return to Georgia.

I phoned her one night asking her what she was doing, and she told me, laughing, that I would be shocked: she was packing her house. It had sold in two weeks, to the astonishment of all the naysayers. When I asked where she was moving, she said, "I think I'll go to Nashville," at which point I asked her how she was going to work with me if she moved that far north of Atlanta. Years earlier when she and Stanley moved to Florida, she always told me that she would return one day to become active again in the business. I remember her saying she just wanted to be closer to her son. I suggested she put everything in storage and come stay with me for a while. It didn't matter to me if it was a few weeks, months, or whatever, until she knew exactly where she wanted to move. She said she'd think about it.

After deciding to take me up on my offer, Sandy moved to Lawrenceville in February, 2009, to stay "a while." What a blessing her presence has been for me! I had never lived alone until Jerry passed away. The house we had shared and loved had come to seem huge, overwhelmingly empty, and barren of any form of laughter or life. From loneliness, I was driving each evening to Duane and Kim's home to stay with them. I liked people being around. Her move has been a wonderful solution for us both. She has been with me for over two years, and neither of us foresees any changes in the near future, certainly. As I always say, "I'm not going anywhere!" Life is good once again.

Duane and me with Art and Angela Williams

Chapter Twelve

Building a Legacy

I have now been with Primerica more than thirty years. It seems like just yesterday I began my career with the company, and I love what I do as much today as in the beginning. It is a great company, offering the consumer valuable financial direction and products. There are those who frequently ask me when I'm going to retire. I respond, "And do what?" If I retired, I'd be miserable and have nothing to do. I understand how an individual working a forty-plus hour week with someone else dictating when to be at work, what to do at work, when the work day ends as well as when the person is entitled to time off (with or without pay) would be eager to retire. I would be, too, if I were in that position, but fortunately I'm not.

As I said earlier, I have always worked for myself. Having been raised in an agricultural family where we made, grew, sold, exchanged, or bartered for what we needed, I learned self-sufficiency as a child. My family made their own way, so as an adult, I have followed the same course. I've always worked for myself, having two different businesses of my own. I am blessed in that I work when I want to, answering to no one, and helping people all the time. Most retired people I know enjoy doing something. They don't like to just sit. They volunteer and help here and there doing different things to stay active. They enjoy helping people. I'm doing the same, but I just get paid for what I do on a continuous basis. Guess I'll just work until I drop.

I am able to offer clients and potential clients numerous financial products for the benefit of their families. The variety of products include but are not limited to term-life insurance, mutual-fund investments, 401Ks, IRAs, long- term-care insurance, and auto insurance: just about anything to do with money. I loved styling hair. I ate, slept, and breathed it. But my work is so much easier now and not nearly as hard on my body. Plus, I am making much more money, too. I found something I like to do as much, if not more, than styling hair. One of the first things I learned as I began to acquire my various licenses and go through training in my new career was the power of time and money. Here is just one example: When a baby is born, if the parents would start a mutual fund for that baby, contributing just small amounts of money throughout that child's life, when the child reaches retirement, he or she would be just fine financially because there is so much time for the money to work, multiplying itself. I am so grateful Duane learned this principle and began practicing it almost immediately and at an early age.

To take my time and money example one step further, let me ask you to consider the following. A one-time investment of $500 at birth, left untouched and averaging a twelve-percent return would grow to more than $1.1 million by retirement age. Suppose it did half as well. Even a little bit of money set aside, left alone for a long period of time, is going to amount to a huge sum over time. These principles should have been taught to us in school. When I got out of school, I went into business for myself and worked ten, twelve, fourteen hours a day. I made good money, but I did everything but the right thing with the money because I did not know basic financial principles. When these simple principles clicked in my brain, I was determined one of my goals would be to become the one in my family to make a financial difference in their future. And I have!

Each of my grandchildren, from the day he or she left the hospital maternity ward, had a mutual fund. There will never be a question about whether they will be able to afford college; the questions will be where and when, not how. If they continue to invest, they will become totally financially independent as very young adults.

Each year as I am Christmas shopping, I observe parents with two or more shopping carts filled to overflowing with toys. I want so much to tell them to put one of those carts back and invest the money instead. It is amazing what people in general don't know and don't realize about how money and time work together. Jerry and I made a decision when our grandchildren were born not to fall into the same trap we had witnessed other grandparents slip into regarding gift giving. Instead of lavishing our grandchildren with toys and games for holidays and birthdays, we elected to designate a certain amount of money for investment. For each child, we would purchase one toy and one new outfit. The rest of the dollar amount we had determined for the gift would be deposited into their individual mutual funds. Every Christmas, they each have a card under the tree with a check in it for their mutual funds, and they open them with squeals of excitement. As they each grow into adulthood, the day will come when they will be really excited when they understand the significance of all the zeros in their account balances.

Chapter Thirteen

My Playmates

Seems I have a natural liking for baby dolls. I always have and still do to this day. I suppose my maternal instincts kicked in early in my childhood. The very first baby doll I clearly remember owning was the doll I desperately clung to at age four, as I stood under the oak trees watching our house burn. For purely sentimental reasons, I wish I knew what happened to that doll. She offered me so much security at that time. After the house burned, mother made me a rag doll I named Goldilocks because of her golden yellow hair, made from knitting yarn. Today she is still with me and sits on the fireplace hearth in my den.

When I was in the fifth grade, I received a beautiful, dark-blonde princess doll with the eyes of an angel; I named her Prissy. She was in a pink voile dress which she still wears today. Prissy is still sitting on her own little chair just outside my bedroom door and greets me each morning as I rise. Can you imagine? Prissy has been ever faithful to follow me through the various stages and events of my lifetime. I suppose, therefore, that she decided years ago that I was not going anywhere, and I have been faithful in caring for her as well.

My love of dolls led me to make creative use of a smokehouse Daddy built in the back yard about thirty feet or so away from the back door. With a concrete floor and window-less walls, the front door to the smokehouse was the only entrance as well as the only light source. Upon entering, there was a partition wall that divided the single-room dwelling into two separate areas. Daddy used the right side for smoking the meats and curing hams while I created every little girl's dream of a playhouse on the left side. I was inventive as well as practical in my décor and interior design. I found an old-fashioned heavy wooden orange crate which I turned upside down and covered with a bed pillow to use as the bed for my girls, Goldilocks and Prissy. I confiscated extra bricks from one of Daddy's previous projects from the yard and built a stove to do my pretend cooking on; however, I never did try to light a fire as Duane did when he was a child.

Coca-Cola crates were not as long as the orange crates, and I used those to design chairs. Whenever Daddy would purchase the soft drinks, which were a luxury in those days, he would bring them home in the now-famous crates. I was the little mama to my girls and followed the example of my own mother as I pretended to cook, can vegetables, clean with one of her handmade brooms, and care for my children. I even spanked them with a switch when either or both misbehaved. A tea set which Santa Claus brought me served as my dishware, and I snuck an extra pot and several utensils from our kitchen. There were always fresh picked wild flowers (and I'm certain some flowering weeds) on the tables made from peach crates. I taught my girls manners, dressed them appropriately, and insisted on lady-like behavior just as I had been taught. I was the perfect mama, and this was my domain.

Several years passed, and I was in eighth grade when I spotted "her" in a Davison's display window while I was in Macon with Mother shopping for Christmas. She was just about the ugliest doll I had ever seen in my life, but for some unknown reason, when our eyes locked together an unbreakable bond was formed. I suppose this is a true example of beauty being in the eye of the beholder. I had a fit. I wanted her and did not stop talking about her all day. I have no idea how mother managed to sneak around and purchase this doll without my having any knowledge of her doing so, but she was successful. What a wonderful Christmas-morning surprise! No one could understand my attraction and devotion to her, but my feelings never wavered. Her eighteen-inch frame was made from a thick vinyl material, her short gold hair was curly all over, and she was dressed in a bright pink outfit. Her blue eyes spoke to me all the time. I named her Ginny, and I loved her without question. I learned to care for her with tenderness as I would bathe her and wash her curly hair in the tub with me. I suppose one might even say my career as a hair stylist began with shampooing and styling Ginny's hair.

Like Prissy, Ginny followed me into my adult life and had pride of place on the sofa in our den in Reynolds. So she, too, was a fixture in our home. Then one day I realized she was not on the sofa. I asked Jerry if he knew where she was, and he did not. I asked the same of each of the children, Duane, Terrie, and Debbie. No one knew her whereabouts. I searched through the house for Ginny with increasing panic, but she was gone, never to be seen again. For weeks I remember hoping she would magically reappear, but this was not to be. I am confident someone knows where she is or at least what happened to her. I certainly don't.One of my heart' desires would be to know what happened to my Ginny before I die. Maybe, just maybe, I'll find out.

When Kim and Duane married, Kim lovingly presented me with a beautiful baby girl named Diana, with a vinyl face, hands, and legs. She is dressed in a long, white flowing Christening gown and a baptismal cap covers her light blonde hair. Her pale skin and sweet smile of tender softness are reminders of the innocence of childhood, perfectly peaceful. I have a cream-colored chair in my bedroom where she rests, keeping a watchful eye over me as I sleep each night. I've often jokingly wondered if Kim gave me this charming little girl, knowing she was capturing my little boy!

In the same chair, I have a Lee Middleton Doll which I bought for myself about five years ago. I simply could not resist him. This bright blue-eyed little boy is dressed in white with a matching white cap. Appropriately named Precious, he appears pristine, although his slightly mischievous smile hints of possible future mayhem.

The most angelic baby of the group is literally an infant, so small she snuggles securely in the palm of my hand. This adorable dainty and diminutive girl came to live with me four years ago. With baby-fine hair and dressed in a white-footed sleeper and a pale pink-hooded sweater, she completely looks the part of a baby girl. The attention to detail of her tiny fingernails and toenails is amazing. I instantly fell in love with "Beth" as her big brown eyes called to me from the pages of the Ashton Drake catalog. I decided then and there she would be a grand addition to my collection. She is about twenty inches tall and sits in the same chair in my bedroom with Diana and Precious. Beth's tightly curled short-blonde hair complements her pale-pink bonnet and two-piece outfit.

The cutest one of the lot is my little newborn, Nina. She is a mere twelve inches long and makes sounds exactly like a baby laughing. Hearing the sweet sound of this joyous laughter, you would swear this was a live baby. You can't help but laugh with her. As she laughs, she turns her head slightly to the left or right and occasionally sighs. She will slowly close her baby blues as contentment spreads over her cherub face, and she begins sucking on the tiny white pacifier permanently fixed to her rosy lips. With delicate wisps of light blonde hair framing her teeny face, it is impossible to resist picking her up to cuddle or to rock and sway to the music of her laughter. My granddaughter Rhys just loves Nina, and for several years would ask me if she could have her. For Christmas 2009, I surprised Rhys with a Nina of her own, and she was delighted.

Years ago, my lifelong friend Shelvie surprised me with a porcelain baby doll she had made by hand; I named her Shelvie, in honor of her creator. She is dressed in white and pink; Shelvie is lying in a white cradle just outside of my bedroom door, keeping a watchful eye on her big sister, Prissy.

By the fireplace in my home, there sits a brown wicker baby carriage which houses three of my porcelain dolls. "Red" has long red curls and is dressed in a peach-colored dressy outfit. "Ruth" has long golden-blonde pig tails which set off her royal blue eyes and green outfit. My friend and business associate, Jeannette, brought Ruth to me one year when she was attending a business meeting here and stayed in the Hotel Happiness.

About eight years ago, Terrie presented me with a beautiful porcelain boy that she made by hand. At about two feet tall, he is "boy" if there ever was one! His blonde hair and brown eyes accent his blue jeans and plaid shirt. True to his adorable image, he is sitting on a blonde-colored wood train in my bedroom. He is affectionately named Jerry.

Chapter Fourteen

The Fab Five

From the moment their fifth child was born, Duane and Kim have called their children "The Fab Five," and they are indeed fabulous in every way. Of course, I am a prejudiced grandmother!

Our next generation began with the arrival of Ramey Kimber, who joined our family while Duane and Kim were living in Atlanta in 1995. Ramey is the epitome of a true Southern belle in all she is and does. Even with all this femininity, she is our resident gardener. She loves playing in the dirt, and each year has a full garden of vegetables and flowers. Her world is brightly colored, sporty, soft-spoken, and delicate.

Kiley Morgan joined her big sister in 1997 while Duane and Kim were living in New Jersey. Kiley is the nature/nurturer. Trust me; this has to be a God thing! She finds the orphaned or disabled, whether they be birds, frogs, butterflies, or bugs and tries to nurture them to health indoors. When she successfully accomplishes each task, she lovingly and tenderly surrenders each back to their world.

Our reader is Ryver Cauley, who arrived in California in 1999. Ryver the Reader is known to sit, lie, stand, or curl up as he escapes into the magical world of the printed page, remaining secluded for hour upon hour as he devours the knowledge he holds in his hands.

Flynt Cayden artfully manifests every conceivable aspect of the Flint River in Georgia, where he, too, joined this ever-growing family. His love of life and ever-deepening belief in the principle of "no pain no gain" has earned him the nickname of "Rock." He is our resident daredevil and fears nothing.

And then, in 2004 the family's most-recent expansion project, Rhys Elizabeth, arrived in true form. She has affectionately become known to us as "Queeny" since her debut occurred while her family was living in England. Her middle name, Elizabeth, is in honor of the queen. Sometimes, her parents will teasingly refer to her as Little Willie; they think she looks like me and even walks like me. Pink is the name of the game for this girl, and she is all girl. However, don't be fooled for a moment. She is perfectly capable of fending for herself. She may be the baby, but she is not afraid to stand up for herself, and she will position those little hands on her hips, shake that tiny finger, and give her siblings or whoever one of her famous "what for" scoldings.

These five look forward to going to the farm, Uncle Will's home place. They each love hunting, fishing, riding their four wheelers, and playing in the dirt with their daddy. They just love good, wholesome, outdoor fun in the countryside.

I am definitely not the norm when it comes to being a grandmother. I wanted the grandchildren to call me Willie. Jerry, on the other hand, was happy with being Granddaddy. Being the independent thinker she is, I suppose Ramey decided Jerry should be "Grand-Jerry," instead of Granddaddy, and it stuck. The additional four have followed suit, and he was their "Grand-Jerry."

I suppose Ramey was somewhere between three and four years of age when I walked into the den one day where she was sitting on Duane's lap, combing his hair. There were a few moments of casual conversation before I pointed my finger at Duane and asked her, "Who is that?" Her eyes brightened for a moment before turning quizzical. A second time I asked, "Who is that?" and again pointed at Duane. She just sat there, not knowing what to say. Finally, I walked over and touched Duane on the shoulder as I said, "That's *my* baby!"

Anyone in the room could have seen the wheels turning in that little mind of hers as she sat very still contemplating what I had just revealed. Suddenly, she perked up and with newfound assurance and glee she boldly inquired, "He's your Baby Daddy?" Duane and I burst into hilarious laughter and, she, realizing she had received such a positive response to her statement, added her tiny shrills of laughter to ours. When I could finally catch my breath, I smilingly said to her, "Yes, Ramey, that's my Baby Daddy." The nickname stuck and to this day, I will often refer to Duane as my Baby Daddy.

My grandchildren have all been born into and grown up in the world of Primerica; therefore, they all have great positive attitudes. They are so fortunate to be Primerica kids. They have lived in many different states and countries, which gave them experiences of a lifetime. Due to Primerica, they know the "Rule of 72," an easy way to figure how long it takes savings to double. (You divide 72 by the interest rate you earn to find out how many years it will take your money to double.) The financial awareness they have due to knowing this rule and other principles may mean that they will never have to struggle financially, and that thought makes me very happy!

I'm extremely proud of each one of my grandchildren. I only wish their "Grand-Jerry" could be here to join in the fun with them, and we could watch together as each one grows in maturity and develops into the fine young men and women they are destined to become. I look forward to witnessing this ongoing process with each of them, because, after all, I'm not going anywhere!

Chapter Fifteen

Yes, I Can

I've always believed and trusted in the power of faith, and it is faith that has literally carried me through, over, and above various circumstances that led me to believe the sun would never rise again. I have long been convinced one does not fully comprehend or relate to the ever-increasing depths of his or her faith until it has been tested by the fires of refinement. While life for me has been good, there have been challenges to face individually and as a family. Again, our sustaining stance is, "I can do all things through Christ which strengthens me."

Kim and Duane were given the opportunity, through Primerica, to move to England in the summer of 2003. They loved it! They were fortunate to live there for a couple of years. Jerry and I went to visit them several times and fell in love with the country, the people, and the history; I decided I could easily live there. Duane writes about many of their experiences in England, the new friends they made, and some of the challenges they overcame in his 2008 book, *Y Not You?*

With each new challenge, our faith as a family has been tried and purified, ever increasing our deepening trust in our Lord and the promises in His Word of His loving care of each of us. This, together with positive attitudes, strengthens our resolve and belief that we don't take kindly to the use of the word "never," choosing instead to believe, "Yes, I can!"

In June, 2004, Rhys was born in Oxford, and as the newest addition to her family, she accompanied her parents and siblings to Georgia for a month-long vacation. As they were packing the car to drive to the airport in England, I had to make a call to Duane, telling him their home in Atlanta had burned to the ground the previous day. As heartrending as this experience was, we all learned valuable lessons, especially regarding what is and is not important and lasting in life. Following their return to England the first week of October, I was busily preparing for a meeting at my office when I received a phone call from Kim. I will never forget her opening question, "Are you sitting down?" to which I replied positively. She continued, "Duane has a slipped disc in his neck and can't feel his legs." Within a matter of hours, the company had graciously made the necessary arrangements for Jerry and me to fly to England; we were on the plane by late afternoon. Kim had barely arrived at the hospital when the medical staff was transporting Duane into emergency surgery, less than four hours after he had collapsed from a broken neck. Word of his condition spread through family, friends, church, and corporate circles as though lightning had struck. Prayers were being lifted, well-wishes sent, phone calls made, and tears shed. Duane had been in the hospital for six days when the decision was made to fly him back to Atlanta to the Shepherd Spinal Center. I accompanied him on the return flight aboard the jet ambulance; Jerry followed us on a commercial flight.

Being quite certain it would only take a few weeks for the injuries to heal and for him to recover, Duane asked Kim if she and the children would remain in England. He did not want to disrupt their schedules or pull the children out of school. Kim's mother, Sandra, had flown to England to be by Kim's side and help with the children while Duane was recuperating. After the strenuous flight, multiple tests, conferences with the physicians, and days of poking and prodding, we sat down to hear the diagnosis and prognosis. He would never again walk, they said. Duane was challenged; he asked the doctors how many of their patients with his type of injuries had overcome their challenge; one of the doctors said three. Duane immediately responded with this promise: "You've just met your fourth!"

Within five days of being at the spinal clinic in Atlanta, Duane phoned Kim and told her he realized this would be far more challenging and a much longer process than he first thought. He could not do this without her, he said, and he asked her to come to Georgia. Kim and her mother made the arrangements, packed, and with children in tow, flew out almost immediately.

We were sitting in Duane's room at Shepherd Spinal Center one morning when a perky social worker for the hospital entered and began asking Duane multiple questions. At first, Duane had no problem in answering her questions, but suddenly he asked her what this was all about. She calmly began to explain to him that she was completing the paperwork necessary to submit to have him declared "disabled." I thought Duane was going to come up off the bed as he boldly declared to her, "I am not disabled. I am not going to receive disability, and I am not going to answer any more of your questions!" Stunned, she turned and walked out the door, and we never saw her again. That's my boy!

While Duane was a patient at Shepherd's, I visited him daily. Cards, letters, prayers, visitors, and flowers poured into his room from all over America, Canada, England, Spain—everywhere they had lived. It seemed endless. One morning, a nurse who was attending Duane entered his room cautiously and said, "Can I ask you something?" Duane's response was, "Yeah, sure," to which she replied, "Who are you?"

Duane, being the good-natured jokester he is, laughed and asked her what she was talking about, and she said, "So many people are coming to visit you. Calls are streaming in constantly. Cards are arriving by the buckets and flowers by the truck loads. We have all decided you are some kind of celebrity or something." We all still laugh about Duane's "celebrity" status.

Duane remained in the hospital almost six weeks as an inpatient. Although Duane was still working hard to meet the challenge of recovery, as he still does today, he and his family enjoyed Christmas with family and friends before returning to England the first week of January 2005 to resume their life. God is good!

By February, we all realized it was not in Duane's best interest to remain in England. After much deliberation with both corporate friends and with family, Duane and Kim made the decision to return to America. Again, Sandra was at her daughter's side, helping pack their house and move the family of seven back to Georgia.

No sooner than they had returned and life began to show some degree of normality, we faced yet another crisis. We were all together as a family, picnicking and celebrating July 4th with barbecue and all the fixings, when Duane suddenly keeled over with intense and relentless pain. He decided to lie down for a while to see if the pain would go away. He was so sure it was only a case of indigestion. Instead of getting better, the pain continued to worsen. He did not want to go to the hospital, but we finally convinced him to let us take him to the local emergency room. Within an hour, the doctors determined an ulcer had burst in his stomach, spewing food and bacteria throughout his internal system. Untreated, he could have died in only a matter of hours. Surgery removed half of his stomach, damaged from the rupture. He recovered quickly, and that was good thing, too, because we were soon to face another frightful event.

The very next month, Kiley and Ramey were playing outside with their babysitter, Kaitlin, and riding their Rhino, a four-wheel-drive golf cart. Within minutes, there was an accident, and Kiley was on the ground. The cart's roll bar landed on her chest and bruised her lungs. She had stopped breathing several times by the time Duane reached the scene of the accident. There were people God had placed at the scene or near enough to the scene who were trained professionals in one degree or another of the medical field. They immediately jumped in, offering their assistance and expertise to help keep Kiley breathing until the trauma team and emergency personnel arrived. It was necessary to take her by Life Flight to Scottish Rite Hospital in Atlanta. The next few hours were tortuous for all of us, and the doctors were less than encouraging. Eventually, she was placed in a drug-induced coma and we all held a 24/7 vigil at her bedside, taking turns talking with her, singing to her, and praying and praying and praying. Kiley's arduous struggle of recovery was long and challenging, but she is a Morrow through and through. Kiley has recovered miraculously!

Jerry's carpel tunnel surgery was our next hurdle. We sailed through that like a breeze in 2006, only to be faced with his diagnosis of ALS in the early months of 2007 and with losing him in 2008.

Some months after Jerry passed, as I was returning home from middle Georgia, I noticed the muscles in my legs were jumping. Suspicious as this was, I wasn't alarmed and thought this would soon stop, but it didn't. I told my doctor about it, and he sent me to a neurosurgeon who, in turn, ordered a brain scan and tests on my muscles. He did not diagnose anything at this time, but scheduled me to return in three months.

Over the next three months, I began walking very slowly and rising from the couch or chair even more slowly. I noticed I was having considerable difficulty raising my arms over my head as I tried to comb my hair. Occasionally, my head would twitch, and my hands would shake almost uncontrollably from time to time. Friends who also noticed began asking me if I had a crick in my neck because I looked like I was in such pain.

During this time I attended my high school class reunion; most of the people there noticed a difference in my posture and stamina and asked me how I was. When the designated three months had passed, I returned to the neurosurgeon. He told me that the moment he saw me walk down the hall and into his office, he knew I had Parkinson's disease. He ran more tests, which confirmed his diagnosis. Thinking back, I realized I had experienced symptoms over the past four or five years. I was sick when Jerry was sick and just didn't know it. My focus was on him. When I asked the doctor how many years he thought I had this disease, he said, "Four or five years, don't you think?" I agreed. Then, when I asked him for a prognosis, he just looked at me smilingly and said, "Oh, I'd say thirty years or so." I laughed and responded, "Well, I may live to be as old as my mother anyway; she died at age 94. I think that would be long enough, don't you?" And he agreed.

There have been some misunderstandings since the diagnosis. One day, two of my co-workers walked into my office, shut the door behind them, and proceeded to lecture me. They lovingly told me I had to get my act together. I was crying and grieving entirely too much over Jerry's death and destroying myself and my health in the meantime. I disagreed with them, trying to explain that Jerry had been gone less than a year at this point, and I did miss him terribly. At my diagnosis appointment with my doctor, I told him what they were saying, and he told me emphatically, "You can go back and tell them they are wrong; this has nothing to do with grief."

I am glad to say that the medications my doctor prescribed for me work wonderfully. Of course, from time to time, there are reviews, tests, and sometimes this medication or that one needs adjustment, but, overall, I don't feel like there is anything wrong with me. In my mind, I refuse to have Parkinson's.

So, the years between 2004 and 2009 have presented my family and me with multiple challenges: financial, medical, life threatening, devastating, and even spiritual. In response, we have risen above and conquered through our faith in Jesus Christ. We have reminded ourselves often that, yes, we can do all things through Christ who strengthens us. Yes, there has been sadness and heartache; yes, there has been loss and grief. Yet, along with these we have experienced growth, renewed strength, revised faith, unimaginable blessings, and an increasing knowledge of who we are, what we are capable of accomplishing, and more importantly, who our God is. Again, I say, "I'm not going anywhere!"

Chapter Sixteen

Moving Forward

Duane has always told me when it came time for him to retire, he wanted to retire in Reynolds, surrounded by the beauty of God's creation. He has such warm and happy memories of his childhood years. Life's pace is relaxed there, the air is cleaner, lifelong friends are still there, together with his "roots and history," plus he wanted woods and pasture. He had told Uncle Will and Aunt Mildred many times if they ever decided to sell their property, to please let him know. The property is located next door to the house I built in 1962, the house where he grew up. As a child, Duane blazed a path from our house to Uncle Will's and loved going there. It was his second home, and although Will and Mildred were not blood relatives, their door was always open, and Duane was always welcomed. He referred to Will and Mildred as his uncle and aunt throughout their lives, and they, in turn, loved him as one of their own. So when Uncle Will's farm became available, Duane and Kim bought it immediately.

The Parks family property consists of a forty-five acre farm, a brick house, and a pool. The grandchildren just love this. There are two ponds where the children love to fish. Most weekends, Duane, Kim, and the kids go down to the farm. The "Fab Five" spend hour upon hour riding four-wheelers, swimming, hunting, fishing, and romping through the woods together, creating memories they will one day relay to their own children and grandchildren.

When Will Parks passed away in 2005, their firstborn child, Linda Grant, together with her husband, Jack, fixed an apartment in their home in Lizella, Georgia, and moved Mildred in to live with them. The Parks had raised their six children (Linda, Wayne, Corine, Joann, May, and Sherry) on this land, but now, it was time to pass the baton. A unanimous decision to sell was made by the family members. When Duane and Kim decided to purchase the farm, they were acutely aware of the Parks' family history and ties to the property, as well as the history they were creating with the Morrow clan. Wanting to capture the past and pay tribute to the Parks family while at the same time looking to their own family future, they elected to name the farm The Morrow-Parks Farm, as it is now known.

In the early part of 2010, Kim and the kids had come over for Sunday lunch. Kim told me that my old house in Reynolds was up for sale. Later that week, the legal notice appeared in the *Taylor County News*. When we moved to Atlanta in 1984, I made the decision not to sell the house immediately. However, five years later we sold it to a couple who lived there for ten years. They sold the house to another couple who lived there a couple of years and sold the house to someone who lived there only a year. Knowing the property joined Duane's property, I decided it would be great to own it again and jumped at the opportunity. I made an offer which was accepted, and the sale closed in May. Almost immediately, Sandy and I began driving to Reynolds each weekend to begin the necessary remodeling project. And what a project it became!

The first item on our project list was to salvage the brick fireplace. At some point, one of the owners had painted the beautiful red-brick fireplace white. I couldn't believe it. A crew of five formed—Sandy, my housemate; Camille, my childhood friend; Jerry's daughter Terrie; May Morga, one of Uncle Will's daughters; and me. Together we worked and scrubbed on that fireplace every weekend for a month, with, of course, all the men around telling us it couldn't be done. We tried everything we could think of to remove the paint from that brick; strippers, water, elbow grease, and muriatic acid didn't touch it. Finally, someone suggested we try Goof Off, and while it still took a good degree of work and an abundance of patience, this worked like a charm. There is now a beautiful red-brick fireplace again. The moral of this story is never, never, ever tell a determined woman what she can't do, especially if she is surrounded by a group of determined women.

Next came the demolition stage, ripping out the flooring, carpets, cabinets, and even some walls. Todd Moore replaced and updated the plumbing, and Michael Lowe brought the electrical system throughout the entire house up to the current building and safety codes. A job for sure! I knew I didn't want the hot water heater in the traditional laundry room as was done in the sixties, but convincing others I knew what I was talking about was at times a challenge. After much discussion and planning, my contractor, Larry Hinton, built a very nice closet in the carport to house the new unit. I had assumed the hot water heater and ice maker would be on the floor with just a covering over them. When I first saw the large size of the closet area, I laughingly called it the "Hot Water Heater Hotel," and the name stuck. This sizeable closet has now also become a great additional storage room.

Every weekend possible from May 2010 through March 2011, Sandy and I would pack my SUV full of needed items and head "down South." Sandy is an amazing packer and can find room for one more item, then one more item, and, finally, one more item. This soon became a standing joke between us as she would tell me not to buy another single thing to take down this week, but, somehow, she always managed to find a place to put my newest acquisitions.

Replacing the cabinets was far easier than I had expected it to be. Sandy's stepson George Gee built beautiful basswood cabinets for the kitchen and bath in his warehouse, storing them there until the renovation phase was completed. He also built the mantle that matches the kitchen cabinets perfectly and installed it over the refurbished fireplace. They are beautiful, and he did a fantastic job. Nothing pleases a woman who loves to cook like a brand-new kitchen!

Brick Barnes has the patience of Job. He has proven he has it, after working with me on the selection of the hardwood floors. I don't know how many samples and stain colors I viewed before making my selection, but there were a lot. Rather than carpet, I had him install hardwood throughout the entire house with the exception of tile in the baths and laundry room. The floors are absolutely gorgeous, and everyone comments on how nicely the wooden floors enhance and modernize the house.

Having built a new house several years ago, my niece Belinda and her husband, David Powell, were definitely experienced and would drop by when we were down there to check in to see how things were going. David is a good man, kind, gentle, and soft spoken just like Jerry. He never gets rattled at anything. He is just a laid-back, easygoing, good soul.

As word began to spread through the community and countryside that I had repurchased my original house, one by one old friends would drop by on the weekends to see the progress, adding their two cents to the project at hand over a glass of *Southern Favorite*'s iced tea. Yes, a few even came to actually work, contributing their expertise and brawn to whatever was going on at the time. Nick Morga, May's husband, was a Godsend from the very beginning as a general handyman, painting, finishing, and doing whatever needed to be done at any given time. My only regret through this entire project has been Jerry not being here to be a part of it. He would have loved to have been a part of this labor of love; this house held many happy memories for both of us, and with his natural know-how, talents and abilities, he could have done much of the work, saving us lots of money.

Throughout the entire renovation project, Sandy and I would stay at Duane and Kim's house whenever we were in Reynolds. The football-field length between the two houses has been challenging to maneuver at times, especially with hands full, carrying things back and forth. As a surprise gift for Christmas of 2010, Duane, Kim, and the Fab Five made arrangements with Santa's clever helpers to design a golf cart painted University of Georgia red with a large *G* on the front.

It enables me to scoot back and forth between the two houses in a moment, easily carrying all I need.

One of the previous owners planted Leyland cypress trees along the side of the driveway. I suppose there were probably eight or ten of them. They had grown to thirty to forty feet in height and were scraggly and unattractive. I wanted to open the area between the two houses and have a clear view of each home. After the entire renovation project was completed, the Leylands were removed, and the difference is absolutely amazing. Let there be light!

Another landscaping project involved a row of red-tips that Uncle Will had planted, probably for privacy, on the property now known as the Morrow-Parks Farm. Duane and I decided to remove this hedge and clean out the undergrowth to make preparations for Duane to have a huge barn built. As with any home, there will always be a never ending to-do list, but isn't that what life is all about?

Over the course of 2010 and 2011, as I have reclaimed my house and completed many renovations, friends and family members have asked if I plan to return to Reynolds and my roots permanently. My response has always been the same. I tell them no, but I add that one never knows what the future will bring, and I like to be prepared. I believe this piece of property is ours, and it was meant to be returned to this family. The land was originally owned by Duane's great-grandmother, Vickie Hartley McElmurray. So, the legacy will continue. If I were to become housebound, it would be much easier for someone to care for me in a ranch-style home in the country, close to my children and grandchildren. In the meantime, I am having too much fun burning up the roads between Atlanta and Reynolds, as well as keeping everyone guessing about what I'm going to do next. And besides, I have enjoyed the way my life has been styled, and as I've said before, "I'm not going anywhere!"

THE END

Appendix

A Note of Thanks Regarding
The Beauty Nook and Jerry's Golden Shears

The Beauty Nook and Jerry's Golden Shears continue to please an ever-increasing clientele. Over the years, we had many shampoo girls (and one fine young man) give the relaxing shampoos while we were cutting, perming, and styling hair. These ever-so-helpful girls and the young man kept us going; they washed and folded towels, swept up the hair we were constantly dropping on the floor, and kept our stations stocked with supplies. Yes, they were at the salon ready to work at 5 a.m. every Saturday, just like the rest of us. Today, these girls love to get together and talk about how strict I was, but at the same time, what fun we all had working together. I owe each one of these wonderful professionals an enormous debt of gratitude for their years of service and friendship. We couldn't have done it without you! Following is a list in alphabetical order by last name of these good Samaritans; I hope I haven't left anyone out.

Hair Stylists

Sherry Barfield, Merita Barrow Carpenter, Colleen Childree, Amelia Taunton Jones, Shelvie Hartley Lackey, Ellen Parks

Locke, Linda Trawick Powell, Carlene Hobbs Rogers, Betty Willis Shiflett.

Shampoo Assistants

Patty Singleton Arrington, Ann Gordon Barrow, Gloria Bazemore, Debbie Morrow Booth, Taron Whitley Bone, Lamar Carpenter, LeAnn Carpenter, Joyce Taunton Childree, Royalyn Waller Crook, Doris Daniels, Kathy Underwood Goddard, Pam Bazemore Harbuck, Gina Hinton, Jane Wilson Hinton, Terrie Morrow Howell, Brenda Arnold Johnson, Jessie Daniels McDowell, Freida McInvale, Sharon Nelson Miller, May Parks Morga, Mary Ann Giles Peterman, Wanda Poole, Beverly Hartley Poore, Belinda Moore Powell, Kathy Nelson Roberson, Lynn Underwood Whatley, and Ann Singleton Watson.